HERBERT LOCKYER

Love is Better

THAN WINE

LEARNING TO LOVE FROM THE SONG OF SOLOMON

WHITAKER
HOUSE

LOVE IS BETTER THAN WINE:
Learning to Love from the Song of Solomon

ISBN: 978-1-62911-815-4
eBook ISBN: 978-1-62911-816-1
Printed in the United States of America
© 1981, 2017 by Ardis A. Lockyer

Whitaker House
1030 Hunt Valley Circle
New Kensington, PA 15068
www.whitakerhouse.com

Library of Congress Cataloging-in-Publication Data (Pending)

1 2 3 4 5 6 7 8 9 10 11 **W** 24 23 22 21 20 19 18 17

CONTENTS

I know not if I know what true love is,
But if I know, then, if I love not Him,
I know there is none other I can love.
—Alfred, Lord Tennyson

INTRODUCTION

*I*n discussing the distinction between a *type* and an *allegory*, Robert Jamieson says that the latter is "a continued metaphor, in which the circumstances are palpably often purely imagery, whilst the thing signified is altogether real."

To understand the Song of Solomon correctly, we must not look for its meaning in *its* allegorical significance, but through the lens of other parts of the Bible. Burrowes views the Song in this unique fashion, "It lies in the casket of revelation an exquisite gem, engraved with emblematical characters, with nothing literal thereon to break the inconsistency of their beauty."

Jamieson agrees with this in a descriptive paragraph:

Like the curiously wrought Middle-Eastern lamps, which do not reveal the beauty of their transparent emblems until lighted up within, so the types and allegories of Scripture, the "lantern to our path" need the inner light of the Holy Spirit of Jesus to reveal their significance, numbers of lovely, sensible and not strictly congruous, but portraying jointly by their very diversity the thousand various and seemingly opposite beauties which meet together in Christ.[1]

Because I have not the deep spiritual insight and ability of Origen (the Greek teacher, writer, and early church father of the third century) to author ten volumes on the Song of Solomon, I am confining myself to an exposition of several of its prominent expressions. May the passages chosen whet the appetite for a more complete study of the Song, eloquent with the truth that the Beloved and His spouse, the bride and Bridegroom, He and she, the Head and the members, form but one Christ. (See Romans 12:4–11; 1 Corinthians 6:15, 12:12–27; Ephesians 4:25, 5:30.)

6

1. Robert Jamieson, *Commentary*, vol. 1 (Hartford, CT: S. S. Scranton & Co., 1871), 415.

Chapter 1

LOVE IS BETTER THAN WINE

Let him kiss me with the kisses of his mouth:
for your love is better than wine.
—Song of Solomon 1:2

The mystical Song of Solomon is full of Christ, but we can only extract honey out its verses if we have sweet meditation of Him whom our souls love. It is vital to cultivate a daily, fresh personal heart-fellowship with the Lord if we would rightly understand this book. It is only out of an ever-deepening love for the Lover of our souls that there can spring consecrated service and a growing delight in all our hands find to do. If we have a passionate love for Christ and His Word, necessary time will be found to show ourselves approved of God.

Let us examine the opening verse, extolling as it does the fragrant love of Him who first loved us.

THE SOURCE OF LOVE: HIM

One cannot fail to notice how abruptly Solomon begins his poem. It has no introduction, but commences with the bride's longing for the one her soul loved so intensely. *"Let him kiss me with the kisses of his mouth: for your love is better than wine."*

Solomon wrote of the pure and passionate love the beloved had for the bride of his choice. During his reign, the king came to experience a great deal about love for and from women—as we know, he had a vast harem. Solomon loved many women from heathen lands and *"had seven hundred wives, princesses, and three hundred concubines"* who turned away his heart from God and caused him to cleave to their idols in love (see 1 Kings 11:1–8).

Through such inordinate love for his heathen wives and their false gods, Solomon found himself rejected by God and his kingdom divided. He never reached the Godward application of the ideal of true love his father David expressed in his tribute to his dear friend, Jonathan: *"Your love to me was wonderful, **passing the love of women**"* (2 Samuel 1:26). If Solomon had experienced the glow of supreme, divine love he came to embody in the thrice-repeated phrase, *"Your love is better than wine,"* he could have easily added, "and women."

In this first verse, the lover does not name the one chief object of her desire. Her heart was full of longing for his embrace, for it was only his love that was better than wine, and his kisses alone she desired.

Jesus, the well-beloved Son of God, came as the personification of divine love and is ever the Lord of love, as well as of law. He not only reveals love but He *is* love.

> Oh! fill me, Jesus, Savior, with Thy love;
> Lead, lead me to the living Fount above!
> Thither may I, in simple faith, draw nigh,
> And never to another fountain fly,
>   But unto Thee.[2]

THE TOKEN OF LOVE: A KISS

Besides the wish of the bride to be with her beloved, the verse is speaking of spiritual intimacy. The Chaldee Version says that in this verse God is speaking face to face with Israel in symbolism, an expression of the close intimacy they enjoyed. Origen paraphrased the verse:

> How long will my spouse send me kisses, or prophecies,
> by Moses and the Prophets! Now I long to have them,
> personally, of Himself. Let Him assume my natural shape
> and kiss me in the Flesh according to the Prophecies.

And what was the Incarnation of Jesus but God kissing humanity in the person of His Son who came as the evidence and expression of His love? In Scripture, a kiss represents:

The Pledge of Reconciliation

That kisses were tokens of reconciliation can be seen in the reunion of Jacob and Esau (see Genesis 33:4); Joseph and his

---

2. Mary Shekleton, "It Passeth Knowledge," 1863.

What was the Incarnation of Jesus but God kissing humanity in the person of His Son who came as the evidence and expression of His love?

brethren (see Genesis 45:15); and the prodigal and his father (see Luke 15:20).

Divine reconciliation became possible when at Calvary, *"righteousness and peace have kissed each other"* (Psalm 85:10). Now it is the responsibility of the sinner to *"kiss the Son, lest He be angry"* (Psalm 2:12).

The Pledge of Affection

When Elisha was called to leave home and follow Elijah, he begged permission to kiss his father and his mother before his departure. (See 1 Kings 19:20.) David and Jonathan *"kissed one another, and wept one with another"* (1 Samuel 20:41).

Judas prostituted this love-token when he betrayed Jesus with a kiss. (See Luke 22:47.) A kiss like his was deceitful. (See Proverbs 27:6.)

It was the custom in the early church to *"salute one another with a holy kiss"* (Romans 16:16). The Ephesian saints *"wept sore, and fell on Paul's neck, and kissed him"* as he prepared to leave them, for they knew that *"they should see his face no more"* (Acts 20:37–38).

The kisses of our heavenly Beloved represent the depth of warmth in His heart-love for His own. Christ loved the church, His bride, and gave himself to purchase her. (See Ephesians 5:21–33.) It was by His death that He kissed her into existence, and His marriage with her is in the blissful future.

The Pledge of Nuptial Contract

It was a touching moment when Jacob and Rachel first met, for we read that *"Jacob kissed Rachel, and lifted up his voice, and wept"* (Genesis 29:11).

11

In ancient times it was an honor if a king permitted his hand or garment to be kissed by his subjects. If he kissed another, mouth to mouth, this was taken to be the greatest of all honors he could bestow.

Mary kissed the feet of her Lord and King, but it is a greater honor to have the kisses of the mouth of our heavenly King, who greatly desires our beauty.

Erskine has taught us to sing: "His mouth the joy of heaven reveals His kisses from above: are pardons, promises and seals of everlasting love."

We are assured that God rests in His love, and we should be found resting in it, too. (See Zephaniah 3:17.) God's love is eternal, unchangeable, without a shadow of a turn; the rock we rest on with confidence; a pillow we may sleep on in peace.

THE OBJECT OF HIS LOVE: ME

Let Him kiss *me!* Do you not marvel that God loves *you?* Paul was filled with wonder and praise as he realized that, although "the chiefest of sinners" (see 1 Timothy 1:15), divine love was focused upon him as if there were no other sinners for God to love: *"The Son of God, who loved me, and gave Himself for me"* (Galatians 2:20). The apostle knew there was nothing in his human heart meriting such wonderful love: such a love became a conducting medium to the love of the lost souls around him.

It passeth knowledge, that dear love of Thine,
My Savior, Jesus: yet this soul of mine
Would of Thy love, in all its breadth and length,

Its height and depths, its everlasting strength
   Know more and more.[3]

May you be found resting and rejoicing in the revelation that God has set His love upon *you* and set *you* as a seal upon His heart! (See Psalm 91:14; Song of Solomon 8:6.)

THE QUALITY OF HIS LOVE: BETTER THAN WINE!

The margin of my Bible has the plural, "Thy *loves*"—meaning that the author is referring to the caresses and kisses of the two lovers. The bride had more pleasure in the deep love of her bridegroom than in the most exquisite delights of sense.

The deep, deep love of Jesus alone can flood the soul with joy and spiritual refreshment. As wine implies earth's best, His love is *better* than the best. Do we esteem it so? Is it true of us?

From the best bliss that earth imparts,
   We turn unfilled to Thee again.[4]

Are earthly friendships and legitimate pleasures the only pure wines we drink from day to day, or is His love better than all such wines? Is the Lord high above all in our heart's affection? Some give Him a place in life—others, a prominent place. May we be found giving Him the *preeminent* place!

3. Mary Shekleton, "It Passeth Knowledge," 1863.
4. Bernard of Clairvaux, "Jesus, Thou Joy of Loving Hearts," translated by Ray Palmer, 1858.

As wine implies
earth's best,

Christ's love is
better than
the best.

Do we esteem it so?

THE MEMORY OF HIS LOVE: WE WILL REMEMBER

Because of the superior quality of the love of the Beloved, it must never be forgotten. Hence, *"We will remember your love more than wine"* (Song of Solomon 1:4). We must never forget His sovereign, immutable, and eternal love, which calls for human love: *"The upright love you"* (Song of Solomon 1:4). If we are among those upright in heart through grace, the love of Jesus should be our daily meditation and constant theme, filling us with joy, peace, and love.

This ever-remembered divine love possesses and displays benevolence. It dignifies its recipients, raising them to glory, honor, and immortality. To constantly remember His love is to find our comfort amid changing circumstances; encouragement in seasons of darkness; confidence in times of trial; inspired fortitude in the hour of danger; patience when burdened and oppressed; submission in grief; and zeal and devotedness in the Beloved's cause and service.

Our daily obligation is to keep ourselves in the love of God and to shun all that is unholy or forbidden. This is enshrined for us in James Montgomery's well-known Communion hymn:

> Can I Gethsemane forget?
>   Or there Thy conflict see,
> Thine agony and bloody sweat,
>   And not remember Thee?
> Remember Thee, and all Thy pains,
>   And all Thy love to me;
> Yea, while a breath, a pulse remains,
>   I will remember Thee.[5]

---

5. James Montgomery, "According to Thy Gracious Word," 1825.

Chapter 2

THE THREEFOLD FRAGRANCE

16

Because of the savor of your good ointments
your name is as ointment poured forth,
therefore do the virgins love you.
—Song of Solomon 1:3

In his "Song of Loves" in Psalm 45, the psalmist depicts our Lord's triple fragrance: *"All Your garments smell of myrrh, and aloes, and cassia, out of the ivory palaces, whereby they have made You glad"* (Psalm 45:8).

The Song of Solomon also contains three fragrances associated with our Lord.

FRAGRANT BLESSINGS: WHAT HE GIVES

"The savor of your good ointments" (Song of Solomon 1:3).

Many Asian cultures are passionately fond of perfumes, so it is no surprise to find constant references to them in the Song. Like the rest of the literature of the ancient world, the Bible often cites precious ointments: see Exodus 30:22–38; Psalm 23:5, 45:7–8; Proverbs 7:17, 27:9; Luke 7:46; and John 12:3 for a few examples.

In our beloved Lord, we have many facets of His sweet perfume. The actual fragrances are used to represent the precious and sweet blessings given to us.

The Ointment of His Love

Like the holy ointment, with which the priests and the tabernacle of old were anointed, the love of God is supreme in that there is not *"any other like it"* (Exodus 30:32). His love, that will not let us go and upon which we rest our weary soul, fills the world with its aroma.

The Ointment of His Spirit

Likened to oil, He is the Oil of Gladness, the Holy Anointing Oil, diffusing divine love and holiness and all His scented fruits: *"Therefore God, even Your God, has anointed You with the oil of gladness above Your fellows"* (Hebrews 1:9).

The Ointment of His Word

What an attar floods the entire book! How goodly and fragrant are its promises! There is no other box of ointment like it to cleanse and sanctify us and to produce beautiful lives.

Out of His pain there came a *perfume* to scent a corrupt world.

His *supreme sacrifice* for our sins had a *sweet savor* in the nostrils of His Father.

The Ointment of His Blood

How rich and royal was the blood that flowed from Immanuel's veins! Out of His pain there came a perfume to scent a corrupt world. His supreme sacrifice for our sins had a sweet savor in the nostrils of His Father. Apart from His crimson blood, there is no antidote for our vileness.

The Ointment of His Gifts

As with the holy anointing oil of old, the gifts of the Spirit are compounded of many spices, as Paul emphasizes in Romans 12—his great chapter dealing with spiritual gifts. While these gifts differ with each believer, they make each life fragrant and fruitful. As no saint is without a gift bestowed by the Spirit, the real question is: "Is the aroma of my gift permeating the area in which I live?"

The Ointment of His Years of Grace

Think of the pure delight of a single hour spent in the presence of our adorable Beloved! When we gather in His palace for prayer, worship, the remembrance of His dying love, and the preaching and teaching of His Word, the whole house is filled with scent. As we come with the incense of lowliness to worship and adore Him, He makes even *our* garments to smell of myrrh.

FRAGRANT BELOVED: WHO HE IS

"Your name is as ointment poured forth" (Song of Solomon 1:3).

Who the beloved, or bridegroom, *is* occupies the central position in the Song. And similarly while what Christ gives is good, beneficial, blessed, and delightful, who He *is* is even more beautiful and fragrant. By His name we understand all that the Beloved is in Himself. He is, in His own person *"a bundle of myrrh"* (Song of Solomon 1:13). The savor of ointments or graces surrounding His *person* indicates all that He is in *character* and *office*, as the One anointed with holy oil. (See Psalm 45:7–8; Isaiah 61:1.) In Ecclesiastes, Solomon says that *"a good name is better than precious ointment"* (7:1), and in its fullest sense this applies to Jesus, who manifested God's fragrant character.

The ointments flowing out from Him are as angels descending from Him. The love of the virgins exalting Him is as angels ascending to Him in wonder and praise. The Giver and His gifts are in complete harmony.

20   The first mention of fragrance in the Bible is in connection with the burnt offerings Noah placed on the altar and which rose to the Lord as a *"sweet savor"* (Genesis 8:21), prophetic of His Son who had to give *Himself* as an offering and a sacrifice unto God for a *"sweet-smelling savor"* (Ephesians 5:2). There was a time when all His scented spices were boxed up in glory, but at His incarnation and death, the box was broken and its fragrance scattered abroad, diffusing His grace.

The psalmist could sing, *"O Lord, our Lord, how excellent is Your name in all the earth!"* (Psalm 8:1). But in Solomon's Song, the chief character has no name apart from *"beloved."* He who is our heavenly Beloved has many names, each with its own peculiar significance.

> Join all the glorious names,
> Of wisdom, love and power

That ever mortals knew,
That angels ever bore:
All are too mean to speak His worth
Too mean to set my Savior forth.[6]

Yet the name loved above every name of His in all courts above is that of *Jesus*, so sweet also in the believer's ear. As Bonar expresses it:

I love the Name of Jesus,
   Immanuel, Christ the Lord.
Like fragrance on the breezes
   His Name abroad is poured.[7]

The life of the believer is a box of ointment, but as with his Lord, the box must be broken. Often sorrow breaks the box, causing the spices inside to flow out for the enrichment of those around.

FRAGRANT BELIEVERS: WHO HE RECEIVES
"Therefore do the virgins love you" (Song of Solomon 1:3).

As it is only from those who are truly the Beloved's that He receives adoration, love, and worship, may we be found with the virgins, loving Him with all our heart, soul, and mind. (See Matthew 22:37.) Belonging to Him who was virgin-born and lived a virgin life, we must have the virgin heart, made so by His virgin blood.

"Virgin" is used in the Bible to symbolize the church's role. As Paul wrote, *"For I am jealous over you with godly jealousy: for*

6. Isaac Watts, "Join All the Glorious Names," 1709.
7. Horatius Bonar, "I Lay My Sins on Jesus," 1843.

At His incarnation and death,

the *box was broken*

and its *fragrance scattered abroad,* diffusing *His grace.*

I have espoused you to one husband, that I may present you as a chaste virgin to Christ" (2 Corinthians 11:2). And the redeemed from the earth are named virgins by John in Revelation 14:4–5:

> ...*they are virgins. These are they which follow the Lamb wherever He goes. These were redeemed from among men, being the first-fruits to God and to the Lamb. And in their mouth was found no guile: for they are without fault before the throne of God.*

Our Lord told the parable of the ten virgins, all of whom loved the bridegroom, even though five were wise and five were foolish. Do we have the inner confidence that we love Him for all He has accomplished for us, and, better still, for all He is in the fragrance of His Person? Is the divine heart pleased and gratified because of our sacrificial heart-love arising and filling heaven with its aroma?

When we read in the Bible from those who walked closely with the Lord, they are never slow or ashamed to express their love.

David's name means "beloved of the Lord," and, true to his name, he could confess, "*I love the LORD*" (Psalm 116:1)!

Paul, immersed in love for His Lord, wrote, "*If any man love not the Lord Jesus Christ, let him be Anathema*" (1 Corinthians 16:22).

Peter had close fellowship with Jesus for three years and witnessed His ascension, yet he revealed his ever-deepening love for Him in his affirmation, "*Whom having not seen, you love; in whom, though now you see Him not, yet believing, you* rejoice with joy unspeakable and full of glory" (1 Peter 1:8). Our eyes have never seen that blessed face of His, yet loving Him is gloriously possible by the Holy Spirit.

John, the disciple whom Jesus loved and who is described as leaning on His bosom, reminded the saints, "We love Him, because He first loved us" (1 John 4:19).

So we learn that love of the Lord determines the quality of our present—and also our eternal—welfare; that it is not sentimental to tell Jesus that we love Him; that our love should not be formal or distant, but as warm and elevating as His is.

As the fragrant Beloved draws near, He asks of each of us, "Love you Me?" (John 21:17).

What inner joy is ours if we can reply frankly and truly, "You know that I love You" (John 21:15). May the breaking of the box of our adoring love at the feet of our wonderful Lord lead to a more complete renunciation of those things He hates, and to a fuller surrender to His blessed will! May the language of our hearts ever be, "My Jesus I love Thee…. For Thee all the pleasures of earth I resign"![8]

> But though I cannot sing, or tell, or know
> The fullness of Thy love, while here below,
> My empty vessel I may freely bring:
> O Thou, Who art of love the living spring,
>   My vessel fill.[9]

---

8. William Featherstone, "My Jesus, I Love Thee," 1987.
9. Mary Shekleton, "It Passeth Knowledge," 1863.

The compelling power of a deep affection dominates the request, *"Draw me, we will run after you"* (Song of Solomon 1:4). We are drawn by His mighty love, as the planets are by the gravitational pull of the sun. Scripture is eloquent with this alluring love of the Lord, which perpetually flows from His heart to a needy, sinful world. Read these incredible words of the love of the Lord:

> *I have loved you with an everlasting love: therefore with lovingkindness have I drawn you.* (Jeremiah 31:3)

> *I drew them with cords of a man, with bands of love.* (Hosea 11:4)

> *No man can come to Me, except the Father which has sent Me draw him.* (John 6:44)

> *And I, if I be lifted up from the earth, will draw all men to Me.* (John 12:32)

I've found a Friend, O such a Friend!
  He loved me ere I knew Him:
He drew me with the cords of love
  And thus He bound me to Him:
And round my heart, still closely twined
  Those ties which naught can sever;
For I am His, and He is mine,
  Forever and forever.[10]

10. James G. Small, "I've Found a Friend," 1866.

Notice how the speaker in the Song of Solomon passes from the singular *me* to the plural *we*—"*Draw **me**, we will run after you*" (Song of Solomon 1:4). While we become the Lord's as *individuals*, we are bound up in Him as a *communion* of saints. No Christian desires to go to heaven alone: "*[Andrew] first finds his own brother Simon…. Philip finds Nathanael*" (John 1:41, 45). Thus, individuality and community meet in the bride, as she is one in the Bridegroom.

The prayer of the bride in the Song is answered beyond her expectation, for she was permitted not only to *run* after her beloved, but go with him into his royal chambers. Eastern rulers admitted none but their most intimate friends into the inmost pavilion of the palace. (See Esther 4:11, 5:2; Psalm 27:5.)

26

Our heavenly King promises to bring us into His banqueting house, and His banner over us will ever be love. (See Song of Solomon 2:4.) The house of many mansions becomes the one, eternal home of both the bride and Bridegroom. (See John 14:2.)

As the "ointment" of the Holy Spirit "poured forth" creates "the love of Christ," may such love be more than ever shed abroad in our hearts (see Romans 5:5), thereby making us more virgin in heart and life—and more fragrant in our witness.

> I ask this gift of Thee,
> A life all lily-fair;
> And fragrant as the place
> Where seraphs are.[11]

---

11. Helen Bradley, "I Am Thine Own, O Christ," 1873.

Chapter 3

THE SUNBURNED SHULAMITE

I am black, but comely, O you daughters of Jerusalem.
—Song of Solomon 1:5

The famous Baptist minister, Charles Haddon Spurgeon, said: "You must have warm hearts, quick sensibilities, lively emotions to interpret the sayings of, and sympathize with, the tender notes of this most sacred song." Ours must be the spiritual intuition, created by the Holy Spirit, if we would rightly unfold its symbolic significance.

In this more difficult passage, the Shulamite and her relatives are prominent, with the Shulamite herself contrasting her lowliness with that of the grace and goodness of the shepherd-king, whose love had captivated her and the virgins. The

As the *fragrant* character of the beloved threw into contrast his lover's lowly personality, so the holiness of our *heavenly* Bridegroom reveals our *unlikeness* to Him.

proper treatment of these verses is only possible when the principles of poetic structure and the features of parallelism are recognized.

HER REALIZED NOTHINGNESS

I am black, but comely, O you daughters of Jerusalem, as the tents of Kedar, as the curtains of Solomon. Look not upon me, because I am black, because the sun has looked upon me: my mother's children were angry with me; they made me the keeper of the vineyards; but my own vineyard have I not kept. (Song of Solomon 1:5–6)

As the fragrant character of the beloved threw into contrast his lover's lowly personality, so the holiness of our heavenly Bridegroom reveals our unlikeness to Him. The nearer we find ourselves to Him whom our souls love, the more conscious we are of our black, sinful condition. Job could confess, *"Now my eye sees You. Wherefore I abhor myself, and repent in dust and ashes"* (Job 42:5–6). So was the effect of Isaiah's vision: *"Woe is me! For I am [unclean]…for my eyes have seen the King, the Lord of hosts"* (Isaiah 6:5).

"*Look not upon me, because I am black,*" cried the Shulamite. Yet although this was the estimation of herself, the daughters of Jerusalem could call her "*fairest among women*" (Song of Solomon 1:8). It is a mark of grace when, conscious of our own shortcomings and unfitness, we become more fair and commendable in the eyes of others.

We are given two descriptions, direct opposites and seeming contradictions in the character of the Shulamite, and in such she is a fitting type of the contradictions always inside the believer.

Her Outward Blemish: "I am black"

The Shulamite was *"black...as the tents of Kedar."* Kedar means *dark*, or *blackness*. These were Arabian tents made of black goatskins, and she uses them as a simile to describe her swarthy looks. This also suggests a contrast between the dark, gloomy tents and the gorgeous state tent in which the king awaited her coming. "The sun scorched me," the Shulamite explains; so her blackness was not natural, but a result of exposure to the sun.

The darkness of the tents of Kedar, however, is symbolic of man's *natural* state through sin. Because of sin, gross darkness came upon sinners, whose understanding became darkened. (See Isaiah 60:2; Ephesians 4:18.) Can we, with Paul, confess, *"I know that in me (that is, in my flesh,) dwells no good thing"* (Romans 7:18)? Too often, we have a self-abnegation which savors of a mock humility instead of true acknowledgment of our weakness before God.

Peter felt how unlike his Lord he was after witnessing His power in the miraculous catch of fishes: *"Depart from me; for I am a sinful man, O Lord"* (Luke 5:8). We are truly blessed if we can sing from the heart Charles Wesley's lines:

Just and holy is Thy Name:
    I am all unrighteousness;
Vile and full of sin I am;
    Thou art full of truth and grace.[12]

---

12. John Wesley, "Jesus Lover of My Soul," 1740.

Thomas Carlyle has the thought in one of his essays: "Always there is a black spot in our sunshine; it is...the shadow of ourselves."[13]

Her Inward Beauty: "I am comely"

While Paul loves to extol the unsearchable riches he had in Christ, he was ever conscious of his spiritual poverty apart from grace. He knew that in Christ he had perfect righteousness, but in himself nothing whatever to merit his salvation. This is why he always used the present tense in describing all he was in himself—"Who *am* [not *was*] the chief of sinners" (see 1 Timothy 1:15) and *"Who am [not was] less than the least of all saints"* (Ephesians 3:8). The Shulamite shared the same estimation of herself in spite of all she had found in her Beloved—*"I am [not was] black."*

31

It is not what we are in ourselves that counts, but what we are in our beloved Lord. The more conscious of what we are in our standing in Him, the more conscious we become of our state apart from Him.

"I am black, but comely...as the curtains of Solomon." What a blessed *but* this is! Black in herself, she yet received comeliness through association with her beloved—who covered her blackness with fine linen, and with silk. (See Ezekiel 16:10.) The comely curtains may refer to the brilliantly colored curtains of Solomon's pavilion with its rich hangings, or to the beautiful

13. Thomas Carlyle, *Sartor Resartus* 2.9 ("The Everlasting Yea"), in *Works*, Ashburton ed., 17 vols. (London and Philadelphia, 1885–88), 3:130: "Always there is a black spot in our sunshine: it is even, as I said, the *Shadow of Ourselves.*"

veil of Solomon's temple, seen only from within. Despite her dark, swarthy appearance, the Shulamite had an unsurpassable beauty, which incensed her brothers. They kept her secluded in case her personal charm should be exploited.

The spiritual application of "black" and "comely" should move our hearts.

"Black" is the symbol of affliction and sorrow. Job laments, *"My skin is black upon me"* (Job 30:30). It also represents the defiling power of sin: *"You have lain among the pots"* (Psalm 68:13). Any pot used for cooking is tarnished and black. Anyone who lies on the floor with them to sleep will wake up covered in the ashes, in the blackness. This is the condition within ourselves. The more we know of the worthiness of our Beloved, the more we discover of our own unworthiness.

"*Comely,*" the symbol of hidden beauty, is what we are in Christ. Although we have lain among the pots, yet we become as *"the wings of a dove covered with silver, and her feathers with yellow gold"* (Psalm 68:13).

"Black" is our natural state, covered, that is, in sin and shadow. "Comely" is a spiritual standing, no longer dark but white as snow through the Savior's cleansing blood, and what we are in the Spirit.

"Black," outwardly, the world does not recognize the attraction; "comely," we are all glorious within. The Chaldee Targum applies *blackness* to Israel when she worshipped the golden calf and *comeliness* to her when she repented of her idolatry. Grace makes us beautiful, yet the sin of worldliness may injure our beauty. The blackness of the Shulamite was occasioned by the heat and burden of the day; and our service cares, and daily toil can cause a swarthy appearance, hiding our spiritual comeliness. May we be saved from having our comeliness turn to corruption! (See Daniel 10:8.)

The word of Jesus is that *"a man's foes shall be they of his own household"* (Matthew 10:36), a rejection the Shulamite experienced when her angry brothers treated her with arbitrary tyranny. The more comely we become, the more unspiritual, unsanctified Christians are incensed and rebuked as they cling to the ways of the flesh we forfeited. Being separated to follow the Lord above all else often involves loneliness. Was this not the lot of Him who became a stranger to His brothers, and an alien to His mother's children? (See Psalm 69:7–17.)

HER PASSIONATE LONGINGS

Tell me, O you whom my soul loves, where you feed, where you make your flock to rest at noon: for why should I be as one that turns aside by the flocks of your companions? If you know not, O you fairest among women, go your way forth by the footsteps of the flock, and feed your kids beside the shepherds' tents. (Song of Solomon 1:7–8)

We now come to the cry of a heart longing for full fellowship with the shepherd-king. If we have a sense of failure, neglect, and unworthiness, the way back is indicated in these verses. Here we have the Shulamite's yearning for the presence of her absent lover, although she speaks of him as if present. Job likewise sighed, *"Oh that I knew where I might find Him! That I might come even to His seat!"* (Job 23:3). What we forget is

Abiding in Him,
we have sweet
communion,
divine nourishment,
rest, and rich
blessings.

that we always find Him where we left Him! Abiding in Him, we have sweet communion, divine nourishment, rest, and rich blessings, just as the Shulamite found in her beloved.

The Privilege of Intimacy: "Tell me, O you"

The Shulamite turns from the daughters of Jerusalem to muse about her absent lover and soliloquizes as if he were present. Her longing heart desires nobody or nothing save the one she loves. What a depth there is in the two pronouns, *"me... you"*! How privileged and blessed to live with nothing between our hearts and our absent, yet ever present, Beloved! What contrasts in the pronouns are brought together—one *black*, the other *beautiful*. This is what it means when we sing:

> My need and Thy great fullness meet
> And I have all in Thee.[14]

Progressing in holiness, the *Thou* comes first. *"He must increase, but I must decrease"* (John 3:30).

The Object of Affection: "Whom my soul loves"

The Shulamite declares her love and purpose to be loyal to her beloved at all costs. There are two references to his love for her:

"Your love is better than wine" (Song of Solomon 1:2). Better than the best joy or bliss earth can impart.

"We will remember your love more than wine" (Song of Solomon 1:4). Jesus said as He instituted His supper, *"This do in remembrance of Me."* The wine now reminds us of His love.

---

14. Jean S. Pigott, "Lord Jesus, Thou Dost Keep Thy Child," 1876.

We have three references to those who love the Beloved:

"The virgins love you" (Song of Solomon 1:3). Without the virgin heart, that is, the pure heart, we cannot love Him intensely.

"The upright love you" (Song of Solomon 1:4). There must be nothing insincere, superficial, or hypocritical in our professed love for Him.

"Whom my soul loves" (Song of Solomon 1:7). The personal aspect of devotion to the Beloved is emphasized.

Interestingly, these three references are akin to the three-fold question of our Lord to Peter in John 21: *"Love you Me more than these?"* (v. 15); *"Love you Me?"* (v. 16); and *"Love you Me?"* (v. 17).

Jamieson suggests that the phrase, *"Whom my soul loves,"* is more intense than *"the virgins love you"* and *"the upright love you."* It is the overpowering love Jesus spoke of when, in reply to the lawyer's question, He said, *"You shall love the Lord your God with all your heart, and with all your soul, and with all your mind"* (Matthew 22:37). Christ claims and accepts nothing else than the undivided affection of those who profess to love Him. The greater our realization of the privilege of intimacy, the deeper our love for Him whose love never fails. Herbert Booth would have us sing from the heart:

Let me love Thee; come, revealing
   All Thy love has done for me;
Melt my heart, so unbelieving,
   By the sight of Calvary:
Let me see Thy love despising

All the shame my sins had brought;
By Thy torments realizing
What a price my pardon brought.[15]

The Source of Sustenance: "Where you feed"

Where else does the Shepherd feed His flock but in the Word revealing Him? If we would be fed, we must follow the Shepherd through the *whole* breadth of His Word, and not stay on *one* spot alone. We have to learn, too, to feed not only on His Word but on *Himself*.

Jesus could say, "My meat is to do the will of my Father." (See John 4:34.) He also taught that we cannot live by material bread alone. If we would grow like Him, we must feed in the same places and on the same food. *"As He is, so are we"* (1 John 4:17). "As living souls are fed, O feed me, or I die."[16]

With the Lord as our Shepherd-Lover, we never lack the necessary, nourishing spiritual food our souls require, as well as daily bread for our bodies. The question is: Do we have the heart-hunger for all He can supply? Are we feeding upon His Word and will?

The Haven of Rest: "Where you make your flock to rest at noon"

We need *repose* as well as *repast*, rest as well as replenishment. We require silence as well as sustenance. May grace be ours to preserve the hour of prayer with the Great Shepherd for devoted communion with Him as a first priority. If we miss Christ either in reading His Word to feed us or in prayer when

15. Herbert Booth, "Let Me Love Thee," 1899.
16. John Samuel Monsell, Jr., "I Hunger and I Thirst," 1866.

we rest in Him, we are apt to lose Him for both. If we forget to walk with Him as He feeds His flock, there is the danger of failing to find His resting place.

At noon! In the East this is the most oppressive hour of the day when rest is necessary from labor. *"A shadow in the day-time from the heat"* (Isaiah 4:6) is what the Shulamite desired to share with her lover. Do we find our work wearisome and our circumstances oppressive? Often we become peevish, irritable, or bad-tempered during the hottest hour of the day or when the crosscurrents of life combine to disturb our peace of heart. Then our highest service is rest, as we find it in the arms of our Lord. Finding where our Beloved feeds, we should rest in Him, who is our *"rest for ever"* (Psalm 132:14).

The Assurance of Safety: "Why should I be as one that is veiled beside the flocks of thy companions?" (ASV)

In this culture, a true bride was not veiled, but a harlot was. (See Genesis 38:15.) Mourners, or unknown women, were likewise veiled, but not those who were glad in heart and fully known. (See 2 Samuel 15:30.) We can paraphrase the question of the Shulamite: "Why should I be so unhappy as to have to long for, labor for you, and yet be out of communion with you, and estranged from your servants?" She did not want the beloved's companions to take his place in her affections. Not finding him, she would wander aimlessly beside the other shepherds, in whom she had no interest.

The thought, *"turns aside,"* implies the danger of wandering away. If the bride turned from her lover, there was no other to satisfy her. She could never be content with inferior friendship.

Many virgin-lamps are going out, for these are drifting days, and we must take care not to follow them. Through listening to the alluring voices of the world and to false teachers, many turn aside. Let us not swerve, but keep our eyes on our Beloved who loves, feeds, rests, and guards us.

> My Savior, Thou hast offered rest:
> O, give it then to me:
> The rest of ceasing from myself,
> To find my all in Thee.[17]

The Tribute of Praise: "O you fairest among women"

The adulation of the bridegroom for the bride appears repeatedly: *"Behold, you are fair, my love; behold, you are fair.... Behold, you are fair, my beloved"* (Song of Solomon 1:15, 16); *"My love, my fair one"* (2:10, 13); *"You are fair"* (4:1, see also 7, 10); *"Who is she...fair as the moon?"* (6:10); *"How fair and how pleasant are you, O love, for delights!"* (7:6).

Black, though she confessed to be, her beloved looked at her inner comeliness and expressed his delight in her. He did not break, but blessed, such a bruised reed, for she and he were one. Blissful union can be found in the words, *"My...mine...his"* (2:16). *"I am my beloved's, and my beloved is mine"* (6:3); *"I am my beloved's, and his desire is toward me"* (7:10).

Is not such language symbolic of the delight the heavenly Bridegroom has in His bride, the church? Because He shed His life's blood to bring her into being, is she not precious in His sight? Having given Himself for her redemption, she is ever the

---

17. Eliza H. Hamilton, "My Savior, Thou Hast Offered Rest," 1909.

object of His love, seeing they are one. Jesus could say, *"I and My Father are one"* (John 10:30). And the same indissoluble union exists between Jesus and His church.

It is because He loved the church, and gave Himself for her, that Jesus desires her to be all fair, or, as Paul puts it, *"A glorious church, not having spot, or wrinkle, or any such thing; but that it should be holy and without blemish"* (Ephesians 5:27). John received the revelation of the glorious beauty of *"the bride, the Lamb's wife,"* composed only of those written in the Lamb's book of life, and wrote of her as being luminous as a stone most precious, as it were a *"jasper stone, clear as crystal"* (Revelation 21:9–27).

Because Jesus and His redeemed people are one—through whom He seeks to display His grace, confound His foes, exalt His name, and satisfy His love—are others following our footsteps and joining His flock, and are we feeding hungry hearts all around us? Does our delight in Him, as our Beloved, express itself in active ministry in His service? *"There is that scatters, and yet increases"* (Proverbs 11:24).

Chapter 4

KEEPER OF THE VINEYARDS

*O*ne of the striking features of Solomon's poem of beauty is the way he responded to every charm of nature. Four times over, he speaks of vineyards. (See Song of Solomon 1:6 and 8:11–12.) The unspiritual are mystified by the Song, and the immature obsess over its message of love. But for those with Spirit-anointed minds, it is a celebratory poem both of earthly love and the heavenly love, joy, union, and communion between Jehovah and spiritual Israel, Christ and His church, Christ and the believer.

A FORCED TASK

"They made me the keeper of the vineyards" (Song of Solomon 1:6).

The absorbing love of the Shulamite for her absent beloved riled her jealous brothers who forced her to care for the vines in

The Master
calls us
to labor in His
vineyard
but never compels us
to serve Him.

the scorching sun, thus bringing about the loss of her personal beauty. He has no conscripts.

All of us are keepers of a vineyard of some form or another, meaning that we have a God-given trust or responsibility. We are not forced, as the Shulamite was forced by her brothers, but we are invited. Here are a few examples:

The Vineyard of the Home

As parents, do we realize that home is one of the most precious vineyards of the world and a sacred trust from God? A proverb has it, "Your house is the best of all houses," to which we must add, only if Christ is the Head of the house and the silent Listener to every conversation. Godly homes are the bulwark of a nation and a vineyard in a fruitful hill.

What a sad lack of spiritual homes there is among professing Christians, who try to help society but fail to set their own house in order! To keep a home as the vineyard pleasing to the Lord, all within it must forsake questionable activities and amusements. Those loved ones in the home who are not saved will never be won for the Savior if a worldly atmosphere pervades such a sacred vineyard.

The maintenance of the family altar preserves a home from forces that would wreck its peace and influence. With the rush and pressure of modern life, it is to be regretted that times of gathered prayer and devotion have vanished from many a Christian home. To have a happy vineyard, parents should also pray and labor for the salvation of their dear ones, for they are their keepers. If Jesus is given preeminence in all things and the head of the house can say

Whatever our daily task, we can make it another fruitful vineyard by our consistent witness for Him.

with Joshua, "*As for me and my house, we will serve the* LORD" (Joshua 24:15), the vineyard will be well kept.

The Vineyard of Service

To everyone saved by grace, the Lord of the vineyard says, "Go, work in my vineyard." What a privilege and yet solemn responsibility it is to serve Him in some capacity! What various avenues of service there are both at home, in our cities, and in other countries. As we labor in our divinely appointed vineyard, we find ourselves well cared for by its Owner.

The Vineyard of the Workplace

Whatever our daily task, we can make it another fruitful vineyard by our consistent witness for Him. Christ once labored at a carpenter's bench, which He knew to be part of His Father's business for Him. No matter how humble the task we live by, we can labor, not only for necessary wages, but for the glory of God.

A CONFESSED TRAGEDY

"*But mine own vineyard have I not kept*" (Song of Solomon 1:6).

We can imagine how sorrowfully this confession was made. As the result of the task imposed upon the Shulamite by her brothers, she was forced to neglect her personal vineyard (not an actual one, or her Beloved, or even her reputation, as some writers suggest).

Her lament is the direct result of what she has just told us twice: "*I am black, because the sun has looked upon me.*" Daily laboring in the family vineyards, exposed to the sun, she lost her natural complexion and became black, or sun-bronzed. Her particular vineyard was her personal beauty she was forced to leave uncared-for. In serving others, she had no time to care for herself.

The application for us is that service involves sacrifice. If we would find our lives, we must lose them, for we cannot save others and ourselves at the same time. The priest and the Levite, religious though they were, saved themselves from caring for the half-dead traveler left on the roadside by the robbers. It was the Samaritan who, moved with compassion, forgot self in saving the man from death. (See Luke 10:30–37.) The example of the Lord of the vineyard who saved others, but did not save Himself, should inspire us to offer Him service tinctured by blood.

Here also we are warned against negligence lest we try to keep the vineyards of others, yet leave our own vineyard uncared for. Scripture affords striking illustrations of this danger. Solomon wrote that a person is mightier who *"rules his spirit than he that takes a city"* (Proverbs 16:32). Yet although Solomon ruled over a great kingdom, he was not able to control his passions, for he loved many women. (See 1 Kings 11:1.)

Judas kept the bag, that is, he was the treasurer for Jesus and the twelve. That was his vineyard. Yet the traitor could not keep his heart from greed and avarice.

Paul wrote, *"But I keep under my body, and bring it into subjection: lest that by any means, when I have preached to others, I myself should be a cast-away"* (1 Corinthians 9:27). The apostle's fear was that, in keeping the vineyards of others, he might sacrifice his own.

All of us are subject to spiritual failure and have constant need to watch and pray. Paul urged those in the Corinthian church to examine themselves to discover whether or not they were *"in* the faith," because he knew that it was sadly possible to work *for* the faith without being *in* it. The tragedy of many in the church at Corinth was that, although professedly Christian, they were not spiritual but carnal.

How even more tragic is it when a pastor or preacher publicly endeavors to lead others to the fountain, yet has a dry soul himself, or when he tries to keep the vineyard of the church he serves, yet has no influence in the vineyard of his own home!

The same danger of failure confronts a singer or choir member who sings with much acceptance hymns of victory, holiness, surrender, and peace, yet has no inward song of personal victory because of some hidden sin or worldly inclinations or backsliding heart.

47

The solemn truth is that no outward service, no matter how successful it may appear, can make up for personal failure or lack of care of our own vineyard. In the long run it is not what we *do* but what we *are* that counts for God; that inner sanctification must be, like the coat Jesus wore, *"without seam"* (John 19:23).

Was it not Solomon himself who, sadly neglecting his own vineyard, wrote, *"Keep your heart with all diligence; for out of it are the issues of life"* (Proverbs 4:23)? If we seek to serve the Lord, it is imperative to give ourselves to prayer and meditation, and cultivate personal obedience and holiness, thereby keeping our own vineyard fruitful and fragrant. At the judgment seat of Christ, the keeping of other vineyards will not compensate for the negligence of our own vineyard.

At the **judgment** seat of Christ, the keeping of **other** vineyards will **not compensate** for the **negligence** of **our own.**

Chapter 5

A BUNDLE OF MYRRH, A CLUSTER OF HENNA

$\mathcal{H}$ow Solomon loved forests, fields, vineyards, and gardens! By the Holy Spirit, what a wonderful picture gallery he prepared for us, full of lovely portraits of Him whom our souls love and adore. A saying that traditionally comes from our Lord reads: "Raise the stone, and there thou shalt find me, Cleave the wood and there am I." Raising the stone and cleaving the wood of imagery constituting Solomon's Song, we do find Him who promised that all who truly sought Him would discover Him.

Coming to the king within his palace, and the presence of his lover there after a felt absence, we read of what he thought of her, and of what she was to him.

While the king sits at his table, my spikenard sends forth the smell thereof. A bundle of myrrh is my well-beloved to

*me; he shall lie all night between my breasts. My beloved is
to me as a cluster of camphor [henna] in the vineyards of
Engedi.* (Song of Solomon 1:12–14)

As the beloved reclines on his couch, the bride's presence is
as delightful to him as the scent of costly perfume. He would
call her, *"my spouse,"* whose garments smelled like *"the smell of
Lebanon"* and who was as pleasant as *"camphor [henna], with
spikenard"* (4:10–15), her love having more perfume *"than
all spices."* So her own estimation of her presence was justi-
fied—*"My spikenard sends forth the smell thereof."*

It is easy to see the counterpart in the anointing by Mary
when she broke her box of costly spikenard over the feet of Jesus
and then wiped His feet with her hair. The odor of the perfume
filled the house and also the heart of Jesus with pleasure, for He
said, *"She has done what she could"* (Mark 14:8).

A BUNDLE OF MYRRH

*"A bundle of myrrh is my well-beloved to me; he shall lie all
night between my breasts"* (Song of Solomon 1:13).

This evergreen shrub with fragrant flowers grows in the
rocks and sands in Israel and because of its varied qualities is
frequently mentioned in Scripture. It was valuable as a perfume, hence, the symbol of attractive holiness, which is also of a
priceless value. *"All Your garments smell of myrrh…whereby they
have made You glad"* (Psalm 45:8). The bridegroom is portrayed
coming out of the wilderness *"perfumed with myrrh"* (Song of
Solomon 3:6; see also 5:5, 13).

In those days, women carried a small satchel of this sweet scented shrub on their breast, its perfume being easily detected by those who came near them. This may be the allusion in the bride's affirmation, *"A bundle of myrrh is my beloved to me."* Such close intimacy evidenced a pure, reciprocal love, seen when John, the disciple Jesus loved, leaned on His bosom. (See John 13:23.) John's epistles, so fragrant with love, show their mutual intimacy.

Myrrh was one of the constituents of the holy incense used in the worship of the Lord (see Exodus 30:23) and employed as a sacramental purification (see Esther 2:12). Myrrh was among the gifts the wise men brought to Jesus, and a variety of the plant was used as medicine. It was this, mingled with wine, that was refused by our dying Redeemer (see Mark 15:23) as He would not "dull either the sense of suffering nor the clearness of His communion with the Father with the slumberous potion" (Charles Ellicott).

A CLUSTER OF HENNA

"My beloved is to me as a cluster of camphor [henna] *in the vineyards of Engedi"* (Song of Solomon 1:14).

This small shrub grows in abundance in Engedi, but is found only there. It is about eight to ten feet high, has a dark bark with pale green foliage, and holds clusters of white and yellow blossoms of powerful fragrance which are known as "the flowers of paradise." (The KJVer mistakenly uses "camphor" instead of "henna." Camphor is an aromatic bitter substance fashioned into mothballs and placed among clothes to prevent their ruin by insects.)

Not only is henna a highly prized perfume flower, but when its leaves were pounded into powder it was used by women of all ranks, and men of wealthier classes, to dye the palms of the hands and soles of the feet. When the powder was mixed with water, the plant supplied a red or orange dye, which can be traced on the toenails of female mummies.

In the narration, Solomon uses the shrub as an emblem of true love. In the New Testament revelation, Christ fulfils all that henna suggests. As our Beautifier, He is "the health of our countenance" (see Psalm 42:11), making unnecessary the use of cosmetics to produce charm and beauty of face.

WHAT THE MYRRH AND THE HENNA TOGETHER REPRESENT

We now consider typical aspects of both myrrh and henna which, when taken together, present blessed dual truths.

The Lord in His Death and Resurrection

The fragrance of the myrrh is produced when the tree is cut or wounded. Then it is that life juice flows from its veins to spread its perfume far and wide. Think of all we owe to the blood of the riven side of the Savior! Myrrh is bitter in taste, symbolic of all the travail that filled His soul. "As myrrh new bleeding from the tree, so is the dying Christ to me," as Isaac Watts wrote.

The cluster of henna, when in full blossom, grows in dense profusion, is beautiful, aromatic, and a common shrub that seems never to be robbed of its life, abundance, and strength. It can therefore be seen to symbolize the power and life of the resurrection of our Lord and of all the fragrant fruits of His victory over Satan, sin, and death. The original word for *henna* is *kopher,* the term used for *atonement* or *propitiation,* and thus an apt figure of Him who is our cluster of righteousness and merit, His atonement making void all human merit.

If the bleeding myrrh reminds us of Jesus delivered for our offences and of our union with His cross, seeing we died in Him, then the blooming henna impresses on us the reality that He was raised from the dead for our justification, that we are alive forevermore in Him, and positioned with Him in His glorious palace.

The Lord's Table and the Lord's Day

In the Supper Jesus instituted, which we call the Lord's Table, *we* have the myrrh—the memorial Feast reminding us of all the pain, anguish, and sacrifice on our behalf.

In the day, *the Lord's Day,* as John called the day we know as Sunday, we have the evidence of His triumph over the grave. The day celebrates His dominion! Because our obligation is to keep both the table and the day, may we not be found walking on one leg, trying to observe the day but not the table. (See Acts 20:7.) As we gather in His banqueting house, His banner over us is love.

> Thy body, broken for my sake
> My bread from Heaven shall be:
> The cup of blessing I will take,
> And thus remember Thee.[18]

"Until the day break, and the shadows flee away, I will get me to the mountains of myrrh, and to the hill of frankincense" (Song of Solomon 4:6).

---

18. James Montgomery, "According to Thy Gracious Word," 1825.

If the bleeding myrrh reminds us of our union with His cross, then the blooming henna impresses on us the reality that He was raised from the dead for our justification.

Our Own Life and Service

Taken together, the myrrh and henna can indicate the two-fold relationship of the believer as the result of the twofold work of the Redeemer. *Service* is what we must *do*; *Life* is what we must *be*—and there must be no contradiction between the two.

The myrrh: Placed in small bags or bottles suspended from the neck, and unobservable to the eye of others, the delicious aroma was immediately detected. In like manner, Jesus dwells in our hearts by faith and is hidden from the eyes of others, yet the fragrance He emits is evident in our holiness of life. The world around is quick to observe if the King dwells in the palace of your soul and mine.

The henna: Unlike the hidden myrrh, henna was used openly, those in the East associating its color with love and marriage. Ladies would carry a cluster of it for other eyes to feast upon its beauty and be charmed by its fragrance. Our ways, words, and works should similarly flow from Him who lives within our hearts.

My bundle of myrrh is death to self through Christ, death on the Cross, co-crucifixion, or as Paul states: *"Always bearing about in the body the dying of the Lord Jesus"* (2 Corinthians 4:10).

My cluster of henna is the newness of life I have in Christ, the victorious, fragrant witness in life sustained and controlled by Him, the risen Lord. Paul goes on to say, *"That the life also of Jesus may be made manifest in our body"* (2 Corinthians 4:10; see also Galatians 2:20).

Within the veil, His fragrance poured upon thee;
Without the veil, that fragrance shed abroad.[19]

---

19. Freda Hanbury Allen, "Within the Veil," 1904.

We can never display the cluster of henna unless we offer the bundle of myrrh. It is all too possible that no lovely, pleasing fragrance is detected by others because we have not faced up to all that the myrrh signifies.

THE VINEYARDS OF ENGEDI

The rocky watercourse where the henna is found, the vineyards of Engedi, is also instructive. It is surprising that this oasis of luxurious vegetation is found on the western shore of the Dead Sea. The name *Engedi* means "fountain of the kid," probably because wild goats and gazelles inhabit surrounding cliffs. It was an area celebrated for its rich fruits and costly spices, as well as its abundance of beautiful and fragrant flowers. Engedi was famous as David's retreat when pursued by jealous Saul. (See 1 Samuel 24:1–4.) It was the site of the ancient city known by the name of "The City of Palms."

Vineyards and a city of palms on the shores of the *Dead Sea!* What a rich truth for our desert lives! Beauty in the place of stagnation and death, fragrance amid all that is foul. Such was Engedi. Around us is the dead sea of the world, but are our lives like the lovely vineyards of Engedi? We may think our sphere of life dull, drab, narrow, irksome, monotonous, unproductive of fruit, a kind of dead sea; yet, by God's matchless grace it can be fashioned into a city of palms. Go out and make your vineyard, whatever it may be—home, business, Christian service—as fragrant as the henna of Engedi. Manifest the sweet excellency of the Beloved, yielding to Him your bundle of myrrh and offering to the world so destitute of heavenly perfume the beauty of the henna of a fully consecrated and surrendered life, thus becoming a fruitful, fragrant vineyard in the surrounding dead sea.

One last thought: one Greek word for *Smyrna* means *myrrh*. John used this word in Revelation 2:8 when addressing the church in Smyrna. The Smyrnan church represents the martyrs, and their fragrance fills the whole house of God.

57

Around us is the *dead sea* of the *world*, but our lives can be like the *lovely vineyards* of Engedi.

Chapter 6

THE EYES OF DOVES

Oh that I had wings like a dove!
for then would I fly away, and be at rest.
—Psalm 55:6

One cannot read the Psalms without being impressed with the fact that David knew a great deal about the characteristic features of animals and birds, and of their symbolic use. Small wonder that David's son, Solomon, became the renowned naturalist all the kings of the earth knew him to be. In this short Song, he mentions singing birds, ravens, doves, sheep, horses, roes, hinds, harts, foxes, goats, lions, and leopards.

Perhaps he had a preference for the beautiful dove, using it six times in his romantic poem. The threefold recurrence of the phrase, *"doves' eyes,"* lends a unity to the book. Naturalists are agreed that doves' eyes possess a remarkable power, charm, and attractiveness. The value of the dove is recognized in Scripture by its choice as a fitting symbol of the nature of the Holy Spirit.

Now consider Solomon's tributes to the qualities of eyes. The sevenfold occurrence of *"eyes"* shows that Solomon, with other sacred writers, recognized the value of vision: that there is a language of looks—an evangel of eyes; the gospel of a glance. The eyes are the *two windows* of the soul, reflecting the inner life and bearing the imprint of character, disposition, desires, and thoughts. Physicians can tell the health of patients by their eyes. The eyes are also the *two gates* to the soul. Just as the heart looks out of the windows, so the world of good or evil passes in through these gates. Scripture recognizes the moral value of the eyes, as the records of Eve, Achan, David, and Israel prove. Let us mine for the meaning of the eyes in Solomon's Song.

THE EYE OF COURAGE

"You have ravished my heart with one of your eyes," or, as the ASV margin has it, *"with one [look] of thine eyes"* (Song of Solomon 4:9).

The word *ravish* means "embolden, encourage, hearten," and can be expressed, "You have put heart into me." At the back of the reference, *"with one of your eyes,"* is the custom of Eastern women to be heavily veiled, unveiling only one eye in conversation. In the narrative, the beloved, departing to his mountain of myrrh, is enraptured, heartened by the earnest look of his spouse which spurred him to declare the preciousness of her love. C. H. Spurgeon was fond of saying: "I looked at Him, He looked at me, and we were one forever." It is comforting to remember that *"the eye of the LORD is upon them that fear Him"* (Psalm 33:18).

THE EYE OF VICTORY

"Turn away your eyes from me, for they have overcome me" (Song of Solomon 6:5).

The phrase, *"have overcome me,"* can mean, "taken me by storm, completely overmastered me," or, "dazzled me." What else could the eyes of deity do, but constrain us to yield? Are our eyes fixed earnestly, lovingly upon the heavenly Lover of our soul? He never has to say to His bride, "Turn your eyes away from me."

We read that *"the Lord turned, and looked upon Peter"* (Luke 22:61), and the sorrow, love, compassion, and forgiving grace Peter saw in the eyes of the Lord melted his heart, and he wept bitterly over his shameful denial of his Master he professed to love. Peter understood the language of that unforgettable look and became more than ever the Lord's devoted follower.

THE EYE OF TRANQUILITY

"Your eyes [are] like the fish pools in Heshbon" (Song of Solomon 7:4).

Heshbon, a well-watered region near the Dead Sea, is noted for several deep wells cut in the rock, the water of which is deep, quiet, and full. Such an unruffled surface is impressive and is a type of *"a pure river of water of life, clear as crystal"* that John wrote about (Revelation 22:1). In this comparison, the beloved commends his lover for her particular and peculiar gaze. John Gay, poet of the early seventeenth century, wrote of "a mind

While we can *merit nothing* from our heavenly Bridegroom, we are *thrice blessed* if we have found *grace* in His sight because of a *life* pleasing to *Him.*

serene for contemplation," and such inner serenity manifests itself in the eyes. Do our eyes show an inner tranquility nothing can disturb? "God be in mine eyes, and in my looking."[20]

THE EYE OF PLEASURE

"*Then was I in his eyes as one that found favor*" (Song of Solomon 8:10).

The ASV translates it, "*found peace.*" This indicates the bride's pleasure, joy gleaming in her eyes, as she tarried in the presence of the bridegroom and felt that his heart was satisfied and set at peace as he looked upon her. While we can merit nothing from our heavenly Bridegroom, we are thrice blessed if we have found grace in His sight because of a life pleasing to Him.

THE EYES OF DOVES

"*You have doves' eyes*" (Song of Solomon 1:15; 4:1; see also 5:12).

This triple occurrence of "the eyes of doves" is used of the beloved toward the Shulamite and vice versa, expressing mutual admiration. Solomon made threefold use of doves as a symbol of love, gentleness, and harmlessness.

"*You have doves' eyes within your locks*" (4:1; or, "*behind thy veil*" ASV) suggests the beautiful bright eyes of the bride as she glances through her flowing tresses, or through the slit in her veil, and meets the admiring eyes of her beloved, who cries out, "*You have ravished my heart with one of your eyes*" (4:9).

---

20. *Sarum Primer*, 1558.

The look of a dove is solid, steadfast, and immoveable. Did not Jesus say, *"If…your eye be single, your whole body shall be full of light"* (Matthew 6:22)? Is ours the single eye? It is easy to tell a shifty, wandering person by a lack of solidity of look, but the eyes that are fixed on Jesus never wander.

John the Baptist saw *"the Spirit of God descending like a dove, and lighting upon [Jesus]"* (Matthew 3:16), symbolic of the love and gentleness of both the Holy Spirit and Jesus, in whom God was well pleased. When Jesus came to commission His disciples, He urged them to be *"harmless as doves"* (Matthew 10:16).

> Come as the Dove, and spread Thy wings
> The wings of peaceful love:
> And let Thy Church on earth become
> Blest as the Church above.[21]

The dove was the only bird of the feathered tribe offered in Jewish sacrifices because it was deemed ceremonially clean. But the bird is clean inherently and strives to keep itself clean: hence the implication of, *"My love, my dove, my undefiled"* (Song of Solomon 5:2, see also 6:9). In the days of His flesh, our wonderful Beloved displayed dove-like qualities in that He was *"harmless, [and] undefiled"* (Hebrews 7:26). And because His own, His bride, has an *"inheritance…undefiled,"* she is blessed of Him as she seeks to be *"undefiled"* in the way, walking *"in the law of the Lord"* (1 Peter 1:4; Psalm 119:1).

As the secret of beauty was found in both lovers, it is evident they shared a mutual chastity, innocence, and purity. Like

---

21. Andrew Reed, "Spirit Divine, Attend Our Prayer," 1829.

the shepherd and the Shulamite, the Savior and His church are one, and the Spirit, the holy Dove, ever seeks to make our holiness in Jesus practical in life.

> I want Thy spotless purity
> Forever in my heart to be:
> A reflex of Thy holiness,
> Oh, live Thy life in me![22]

"My love.... O my dove, that are in the clefts of the rock" (Song of Solomon 2:13, 14). Stability of character is suggested here. The bride had only one love, her beloved, and was firm, immoveable in her affection and admiration for him. We sing loudly, "Thou blest Rock of Ages, I'm hiding in Thee!"[23] But are we as rock-like in our love and devotion to the Lord as we should be?

65

There is more of the devil than the dove in our look when we think of family, business, church, political, and theological arguments and disagreements. May the heavenly Dove fill our hearts and eyes with adoring love for the Lord and for others and baptize us with the gentleness that can make us great!

"Like doves beside the water-brooks, washed with milk, and fitly set" (5:12 ASV). Here the lovely, loving dove is bathing in clear waters, then appearing as a shining, sparkling whiteness or glitter as if it had washed in milk. The psalmist beseeched the Lord to wash him until he was whiter than snow. We have the constant need of cleansing from all filthiness of the flesh. Also, the eyes of the Beloved became bright and lustrous as when

---

22. Harry Anderson, "Savior, I Want Thy Love to Know," date unknown.
23. William O. Cushing, "Hiding in Thee," 1876.

Like the **shepherd** and the Shulamite,

the **Savior** and His church are one,

and the Spirit,

the **holy Dove,**

ever seeks to **make our** holiness in Jesus practical in life.

bathed in a river, shining as with passing tears of compassion, as he beheld his loved one. His tears were as precious stones set in a ring.

Isaiah speaks twice of the melting, mournful eye of the dove: "*I did mourn as a dove: mine eyes fail with looking upward*" and "*We...mourn sore like doves*" (Isaiah 38:14; 59:11). Tennyson has the phrase, "the moan of doves in immemorial elms." Because of its plaintive cry, Arabs call the dove, "the daughter of mourning." Its sorrowful note was reckoned to be the mournful repentance of Israel. (See Zechariah 12:10–12.)

A dove is ever faithful to its mate to death, and home-loving, which is the secret of the success of the training of carrier pigeons, the family to which doves belong. A friend of mine, a great pigeon lover, will take one from its nest for a distance of many miles and then release it. Such is its God-given instinct that, once liberated and getting the homeward scent, it will fly nonstop over the miles until back again with its mate. If, because it is weak and the flight too arduous, it dies on its journey home, then its mate sits in solitary sorrow until the end of its life. What a lesson this is for our heavily divorced age and the growing custom of living with successive mates without marriage.

The eyes of Jesus, reflecting the gentleness and innocence of the dove, were similarly sometimes mournful. Often His eyes had tears over the virgin daughter of His people. (See Jeremiah 14:17; Luke 19:41.)

That God's heavenly Dove, the Holy Spirit, can be made to mourn because of men's sin is evident from Paul's injunction, "*Grieve not the Holy Spirit of God*" (Ephesians 4:30).

May our eyes be filled with mourning, sorrow, and compassion as we look upon a world so far from God! There are not enough tears shed over this poor, devil-driven age of ours. Like Jesus, may we see the sins of the town or city in which we live and weep over the sinners.

The beautiful eyes of the Eastern dove are wonderful in that they are able to discern an immense stretch from their cliff nest. Isaiah reminded the saints of his time, *"Your eyes shall see the king in His beauty: they shall behold the land that is very far off"* (Isaiah 33:17). Is ours this distant heavenly vision? Have we the watcher's eye, waiting for the dawning of the coming morn of glory? Are we not encouraged to endure, *"as seeing Him who is invisible"* (Hebrews 11:27)?

68

For a remedy of its ills, the world has its eyes fixed on politics, ethics, uniting nations, brotherhood of man, and recognition of human rights. John Bunyan describes the man whose eyes "could look no way but downwards, with a muck rake in his hand."

With the Bible in our hands, we can lift up our eyes toward heaven, for our help comes from Jehovah. (See Psalm 121:1–2.) Paul had the distant vision of dove's eyes because he pressed toward the prize in glory. His eyes were ever filled with the coming of his Beloved, whose love was better than wine to his heart.

> Turn your eyes upon Jesus,
> Gaze full in His wonderful face:
> And the things of earth will grow strangely dim,
> In the light of His glory and grace.[24]

---

24. Helen H. Lemmel, "Turn Your Eyes upon Jesus," 1922.

Chapter 7

A CHARMING VOICE

*T*he second chapter of Solomon's love poem is conspicuous for its beautiful expressions of true affection. The endearing term, *"my beloved,"* occurs six times in its seventeen verses, and *"my love,"* four times, which gives the chapter a fragrance all its own.

"The voice of my beloved!" (Song of Solomon 2:8). What an arresting, forceful phrase this is, drawing attention to something unique! The words are put in bold relief, as if the *"voice"* was the most outstanding part, and to her heart it was. For her there was no other voice like his, so sweet, musical, charming, and welcome. John Milton thus described Adam's fall in *Paradise Lost:*

> The angel ended, and in Adam's ear
> So charming left his voice, that he awhile
> Thought him still speaking, still stood fixed to hear.

The deeper, fuller, and more intimate our acquaintance with the Lord, the more easily we are able to detect the accents of His voice.

Alexander Pope in *Odyssey* expresses it similarly:

He ceased: but left so charming on their ear
His voice, that listening still they seemed to hear.

The beloved's voice, so vibrant with love, made every fiber of the bride's being quiver, the sound as the strings of a harp under a master touch, magical in its power. She had ears for only one voice as he called over the hills of his coming to her.

The application of the beloved's unforgettable, unsurpassing voice is surely the most wonderful voice of our heavenly Beloved. It thrills the inmost soul, transforms the life.

There is no voice like the voice of Jesus,
Tender and sweet its chime;
Like the musical ring of a flowing spring
In the bright summer time.[25]

Let us consider some aspects of the voice of the Shulamite's shepherd-lover in the Song:

A VOICE SHE KNEW

The maiden was swift to hear and quick to recognize the sound of the voice of the one she adored. It was thus with Mary, who was thrilled as her risen Lord uttered her name.

Acquaintance with the Speaker

We cannot recognize the gentle voice of the beloved Lord unless we know Him as our personal Savior. The Shulamite had previously met her lover under the apple tree. (See Song of

25. W. E. Littlewood, "There Is No Love Like the Love of Jesus," 1857.

Solomon 8:5.) We first meet our Beloved at the tree on which He died for us, and thereafter comes the love covenant. As our Shepherd, He ever goes before us and we follow, for we *"know his voice"* and avoid completely *"the voice of strangers"* (John 10:4–5).

> He drew me, and I followed on,
> Charmed to confess the voice divine.[26]

Although the Bridegroom is hidden from us for the time being, we can hear His voice and our joy abounds. (See John 3:29.) It is said of Moses that the Lord spoke to him *"face to face, as a man speaks to his friend"* (Exodus 33:11). The deeper, fuller, and more intimate our acquaintance with the Lord, the more easily we are able to detect the accents of His voice.

A Trained Ear

The ear of the Shulamite was trained to know the voice of her beloved the instant he spoke. Old Eli knew the voice of the Lord, but young Samuel had to be trained to listen for it. Do we train our ears to listen and thus more quickly discern when He speaks to us through His Word? Do we sit in silence alone with Him and daily train our ears to be alive and quick to catch the least whisper of His voice?

What a beautiful phrase that is in the life of aged Samuel, *"The LORD had told Samuel in his ear a day before Saul came"* (1 Samuel 9:15). It was the Eastern custom to lift the flowing hair covering the ear and whisper the message no other person could hear. Blind Isaac's dilemma was that he knew only too well Jacob's voice but was puzzled by his Esau-like smell and

---

26. Philip Doddridge, "O Happy Day that Fixed My Choice," 1755.

hair. (See Genesis 27:22.) But no such dilemma is ours, for the voice and fragrance of our Beloved are unmistakable, as He whispers to us His secrets.

Hushed Voices

The ardent lover demanded that all other voices cease so that she could hear and concentrate upon the voice of her beloved. Often the Lord speaks to us, but in vain. Other voices, loud and rude, clamor for, and capture, our attention. How insistent are the voices of gain, honor, pleasure, sin, ease, business, human affections, and cares of life; they prevail, as did voices of the priests and people against the voice of Pilate, willing to release Jesus whose voice was soon to be silenced. (See Luke 23:23.) In our hearts may His voice prevail, silencing siren voices and quieting the seductive influences of the world.

73

> Speak Lord in the stillness
> While I wait on Thee:
> Hushed my heart to listen
> In expectancy.[27]

Immediate Obedience

It was because of the love of her heart for her beloved that the Shulamite instantly obeyed the voice that had captivated her. To hear and to hearken to anyone's voice was to obey the law. (See Exodus 15:26.) A common saying of Pliny the Younger was, "The living voice moves"—meaning that the speaking voice affects men more than the voice of words on a page. If we fail to obey promptly, as our divine Bridegroom speaks to our conscience, we lose the

27. Emily May Grimes, "Speak Lord in the Stillness," 1920.

power to know His voice. As He speaks to us through the Word, either in correction or commendation, may we learn to say, "Yes, Lord." The more quickly we obey, the more quickly we discern His voice. When Joshua heard the divine voice, he immediately obeyed. (See Joshua 5:14.)

Have you heard His voice calling you to a deeper life, to separation, to baptism? Then, *"Whatsoever He says to you, do it"* (John 2:5).

Later on in the Song we read the words, *"It is the voice of my beloved that knocks, saying, Open to me"* (5:2). The voice that knocks! Yes, it sounds strange, but His Word is His voice, and it knocks, calling upon us to open every part of our being to His appeal for fuller obedience.

The Shulamite could say, *"The companions hearken to your voice"* (8:13). Is this not similar to the New Testament word, *"My sheep hear My voice…and they follow Me"* (John 10:27)? These are days of strange voices of religious cults, and only the loving, cultivated, and obedient ear can detect their falsity and remain true to the voice of the Beloved. Why, when He utters His voice, even the earth melts. (See Psalm 46:6.)

> Oh, give me Samuel's ear.
> The open ear, O Lord!
> Alive and quick to hear
> Each whisper of Thy Word!
> Like him to answer at Thy call,
> And to obey Thee first of all.[28]

---

28. James Drummond Burns, "Hushed was the Evening Hymn," 1857.

A VOICE SHE LOVED

I overheard a woman say of a well-known radio personality, "Oh, I do love his voice!" Yet she had no contact with the broadcaster and no affection for him. Not so the bride *"My beloved is mine and I am his."*

The attachment we have to a person determines the pleasure we have in the sound of his voice. In the Song the maiden calls the owner of the sweet voice her lover and friend, her affianced, and such praise silenced the daughters of Jerusalem. To her, his love was as strong as death and of such value that it could not be bought. (See 8:6–7.)

Both bride and bridegroom feasted abundantly at the betrothal feast and then slept soundly. The bride then awoke, and she heard the voice of her bridegroom asking her to open the door, addressing her endearingly, *"sister, my love, my dove, my undefiled"* (5:2). Does not our Beloved say, *"Behold, I stand at the door, and knock: if any man hear My voice, and open the door, I will come in to him, and will sup with him, and he with Me"* (Revelation 3:20)? May He enter and enrich your life with His abundance.

If we have heard the voice of Jesus say, *"Come to Me…and…rest"* (Matthew 11:28), and have been enraptured by the voice and message, our praise will be of Him, who is chiefest of all the world beside. Robert Herrick, quaint poet of the seventeenth century, wrote:

So smooth, so sweet, so silv'ry in thy voice,
But listen to thy melting melodious words.

75

Such were the words of One who spoke as no other man and whose voice was as the sound of many waters. We can think of His much-loved voice in its severity, its sympathy, and its symphony.

Its Severity

In the days of His flesh, that voice of His was often laden with righteous anger, as when He compelled the traders to take the doves from the temple or when He called the Pharisees *"whited sepulchers"* (Matthew 23:27) or described Herod as a *"fox"* (Luke 13:32). When we are disobedient to His tender voice, He reproves and corrects us.

> Do you think He ne'er reproves me?
> What a false Friend He would be.[29]

Its Sympathy

The beloved asked of his lover, *"Let me hear your voice; for sweet is your voice"* (Song of Solomon 2:14). She could say of him, *"His fruit* [is] *sweet to my taste"* (2:3). Not only was her face comely, but also her speech. (See 4:3.) Her beloved begs her to lay aside her coyness as she tries to hide herself like a dove in an inaccessible mountain gorge and charm him anew with her rich, soothing voice. She could praise him for his voice, but now *her* voice, although tremulous, is sweet to him.

> Lord, speak to me, that I may speak,
> In living echoes of Thy tone.[30]

---

29. Ellen Lakshmi Goreh, "In the Secret of His Presence," 1883.
30. Frances R. Havergal, "Lord, Speak to Me That I May Speak," 1872.

The Gospels show that Christ's voice possessed loving, consoling, and sympathetic accents, reaching the deepest need of the heart, as when His soothing tone spoke to Mary, *"Why weep you?"* (John 20:15).

Harriet Auber's great hymn on the Holy Spirit carries the verse summarizing the influence of His voice:

And His that gentle voice we hear,
  Soft as the breath of even,
That checks each thought, that calms each fear,
  And speaks of heaven.[31]

Its Symphony

The human voice has remarkable power in that it can sway multitudes as it unites and sings in perfect harmony the notes of a song. The psalmist tells us, *"He does send out His voice, and that a mighty voice"* (Psalm 68:33). There is no other voice like His, able to take the notes of love, grace, mercy, pardon, and righteousness and blend them into one blessed whole. Its melodious music rings through the chambers of our being, assuring us that He is ours and we are His, not for time alone but for all eternity.

A VOICE SHE EXPECTED

In the second idyll a time of reunion after a period of separation is narrated. The Shulamite is stirred by the alluring voice of her beloved she had patiently waited to hear. Tennyson famously wrote:

31. Harriet Auber, "Our Blest Redeemer, Ere He Breathed," 1829.

"Behold he comes!" foreshadows the joyful exclamation of our Great Shepherd's return, as He promised: "I will come again."

O for the touch of a vanish'd hand,
And the sound of a voice that is still.

The Shulamite exclaims with equal feeling: *"The voice of my beloved! behold, he comes leaping upon the mountains, skipping upon the hills"* (2:8). The beloved had been at rest, and the Shulamite did not wish him to be disturbed *"till he [should] please"* (2:7). But suddenly he awakes and comes swiftly to her, hills and mountains being no obstacle to him.

"Behold he comes!" This foreshadows the joyful exclamation of our Great Shepherd's return, as He promised: *"I will come again"* (John 14:3). And when He does so, all mountain hindrances will not deter Him. We shall hear His voice calling us to rise and come away.

As the maiden sighed for the first coming of her lover (see Song of Solomon 2:8), she concludes by praying for his second coming: *"Make haste, my beloved"* (8:14). How blessed to know, and believe, that our Beloved is coming the second time for our complete deliverance from the presence of sin in this dark world. (See John 3:29.)

We read of the departure of the Shulamite from the fascinating court to meet her lover from whom she had been parted: *"My beloved spoke, and said to me, Rise up, my love, my fair one, and come away"* (Song of Solomon 2:10). In some cases *voice* and *hark* are the same in the original, as in "[Hark!] *your brother's blood cries...from the ground"* (Genesis 4:10). So it is with "[Hark!] *my beloved...comes leaping upon the mountains"* (Song of Solomon 2:8).

The voice can also be equivalent to the footsteps of the Lord. Genesis 3:8 records, *"They heard the voice of the LORD God walking in the garden."* How true this is of Christ, whose voice we shall actually hear and whose pierced feet we shall see when He appears saying, *"Rise up, my love, my fair one, and come away"* (2:10).

Isaac Watts taught the bride to sing

The Voice of Beloved sounds
Over the rocks and rising sounds:
O'er the hills of guilt and seas of grief,
He leaps, he flies to my relief.

The bridegroom begs his bride to sing with that sweet voice of hers yet again. (See Song of Solomon 2:14.) The companions also, the young men attending the bridegroom all through the betrothal festivities (see Judges 14:11), were eager to hear her voice. Previously, she had not kept her vineyard, but now she dwells in it and therein yearns for her beloved's voice: *"Cause me to hear it"* (Song of Solomon 8:12, 13).

Can we not put the same language in the lips of our beloved Bridegroom, "Cause Me to hear your voice"? If we know and love Him, He expects to hear our voice of penitence, vibrating with sorrow over sin, our voice of prayer, praise, and testimony ever sweet to Him. Our tones may be weak and trembling, yet His dear voice assures us that He is ours, and we are His. He hears many voices, harsh, jarring, rebellious to His gracious, loving ear. May our voice be sanctified and ever used to magnify His blessed name!

Take my voice and let me sing,
Always, only for my King.
Take my lips and let them be
Filled with messages from Thee.[32]

In Solomon's ode to spring the beloved whispered in the ear of his lover as he came swiftly to her and invited the bride to accompany him to the open country where the air was fresh and laden with the sweet scents of spring. It is here that she will hear the singing of the birds after their silence through the winter. (See Song of Solomon 2:10–13.) Shakespeare has the phrase, "Love, whose month is May." This must have been the sentiment of the beloved when he asked the bride to listen to another voice, the voice of the turtledove, on that beautiful spring day.

In the natural world, spring is the time of revival, bringing with it the prospect of a glorious summer. In the spiritual world the voice of God's Dove, the Holy Spirit, indicates a mighty quickening of the life of the church, after a period of stagnation and deadness.

Think of Pentecost, when through the coming of God's holy, heavenly Dove, the Holy Spirit, a marvelous, exhilarating spiritual upheaval changed the church that Jesus founded into a formidable force!

32. Frances R. Havergal, "Take My Life and Let It Be," 1874.

Chapter 8

GLIMPSES OF THE BRIDEGROOM

Behold, he standeth behind our wall; he looketh in at the windows; he glanceth through the lattice.
—Song of Solomon 2:9 ᴀꜱᴠ

The language suggests that the bride, absent for a while, returns home to find the bridegroom patiently waiting to welcome her.

STANDS BEHIND OUR WALL

This was the stone wall beside the gates through which her beloved appeared and disappeared. The plural *"our"* implies their mutual property, and possibly of their own creation. There is the wall of sin and unbelief, separating God and man, yet He stands beside it, for no wall can keep Him away. (See Isaiah 59:1–2.) He can leap over all our self-built walls, for He longs to forgive and possess us and build around us the wall of salvation. He often stands near when our sin hides Him from us. (See Genesis 28:16; Revelation 3:14–20.)

LOOKS IN AT THE WINDOWS

Such an eager attitude indicates that the beloved was outside looking *in* to catch a glimpse of his love. Although unbelief may keep Christ out of one's soul, He knows all that goes on within it and awaits the opening of the door to let Him in. What do His holy eyes see as they gaze in at the windows of your soul? Is all glorious within through His matchless grace? When He finally enters a life, He closes the door behind, and the open window symbolizes our constant meditation of Him. (Think, for example, of Daniel who always kept his window opened toward Jerusalem, according to Daniel 6:10).

GLANCES THROUGH THE LATTICE

The King James Version has it, "*shewing himself*," the margin says, "flourisheth himself," or, "look bright," and literally means a flower bud bursting forth into glorious bloom. The eyes of the beloved sparkled with delight as he peered through the lattice and saw his spouse approaching. In the absence of glass, the lattice was composed of a series of closely crossed pieces which served as a protection and also as a screen from the glaring sun. These unglazed latticed oriental windows admitted air and a softened light, allowing those within to see out but preventing their being observed from outside. Thus, while the beloved saw

Every part of the inspired Word of God can be compared to windows of beautiful work through which the glory of our Beloved is seen.

the Shulamite approaching, she did not see him, although intuitively she knew he eagerly awaited her.

How sweetly suggestive is this of Him who ever sees the returning prodigal from afar off! Do we catch a glimpse of His holy eyes as they look through the lattice at us? How willing He is to reveal to loving hearts the wealth of His character, the glory of His person, and the riches of His grace! *"He that loves Me shall be loved of My Father, and I will love him, and will manifest Myself to him"* (John 14:21). It is the blessed ministry of the Holy Spirit to show us Jesus as He stands behind the lattice.

LATTICE OF THE SCRIPTURES

What is the Bible but the wall its Author stands behind, the window He looks through, the lattice He reveals himself through to His own and to the world? Every part of the inspired Word of God can be compared to windows of beautiful work through which the glory of our Beloved is seen. Did not He himself say, *"In the volume of the book it is written of Me"* (Hebrews 10:7; see also Psalm 40:7)?

Figures of Christ in the Law

The ancient Levitical Law is called a *"wall of partition"* and a *"veil"* (Ephesians 2:14; 2 Corinthians 3:13), and He is seen standing behind. Old Testament saints knew He was near them, although not clearly seen. Yet the substance was not far from the shadow. (See Colossians 2:17.) Jesus could testify, *"Moses… wrote of Me"* (John 5:46). And Abraham rejoiced to see Christ's day. (See John 8:56.) They saw Him looking through the windows of the ceremonial institution and smiling through the lattice, encouraging their longings for His coming.

Thus the ceremonies and sacrifices were old openings through which the Beloved is seen by those who love Him. Through His cross, all walls were broken down, and through the rent lattice of His flesh there is now nothing between for all who seek to find Him.

Feelings of Christ in the Poetical Books

Job, David, and Solomon all saw the coming Messiah with the eye of faith; they saw Him behind the lattice. Job prayed, *"That which I see not teach You me"* (Job 34:32). And as he peered through the window of revelation, he saw Jesus as the *"daysman"* (Job 9:33) between God and himself and also as the *"redeemer"* (Job 19:25) with whom he would finally stand. David's foreshadowing of Jesus was unique. The psalmist saw His day and was glad. No one can live in the Psalms, especially Psalm 22, and not see Jesus. Solomon, endowed with heavenly wisdom, predicted the inner beauty and glory of Jesus as the coming Bridegroom.

Facts of Christ in the Gospels

Saints, like Simeon and Anna, had a clear vision of Him who was coming as the Savior of the world. And through the four windows of the Gospels and the lattice work of their story, we see the promised One becoming flesh and dwelling among men. Although He came with the glory as of the only Begotten and Beloved One of the Father, the world saw the *Man* Christ Jesus. The lattice of His flesh concealed the Godhead dwelling within. Those on the Mount of Transfiguration beheld His glory flashing through the wall of His body, the window of His flesh, and the lattice of His humanity. All four Gospels end with the accomplishment of His redemptive work for which He was born.

Fruits of Christ in the Acts and Epistles

The Acts and Epistles have a fuller glimpse of Him as the One alive forevermore, interceding on our behalf. This section of the New Testament teaches that the cross is now the window through which He, and we, look out upon a lost world. The wall separating God and the sinner was broken down at Calvary. So we sing:

> Through lattices that light divide
>   Through glorious Gospel lines,
> Through veil of flesh, through pierced side
>   His love, His beauty shines.[33]

Although we live in the dispensation of the revelation and manifestation of a crucified, risen, and glorified Lord, the vision at best is but partial. Now we see through the glass darkly, but when He comes, there will be no intervening lattice, for we shall see Him face to face. Now we see Him through the latticed windows of faith and love and endure, *"as seeing Him who is invisible"* (Hebrews 11:27). Our own mortal condition, the flesh, is a wall between, and we must strive more prayerfully for clearer and more frequent, abiding glances of Him by the eye of faith and heart of love. Paul reminds us that behind the lattice of the table, through the bread and wine, Jesus waits to show Himself to His own blood-washed children. As Horatius Bonar expresses it in his Communion hymn:

> This is the hour of banquet and of song:
>   This is the heavenly table spread for me;

87

---

33. Ralph Erskine.

Behind the lattice of the table, through the bread and wine, Jesus waits to show Himself to His own blood-washed children.

Here let me feast, and feasting, still prolong
  The brief bright hour of fellowship with Thee.[34]

Fullness of Christ in the Revelation

In the song of Deborah and Barak, we read of the mother of Sisera looking out of a window and crying through the lattice, *"Why is his chariot so long in coming?"* (Judges 5:28). But in the last book of the Bible the promised King rides magnificently in His chariot. Thus the book is rightly named the Revelation of Jesus Christ. He comes fully to view as the King of Kings and Lord of Lords. All walls, windows, and lattices are gone, the vision John had being so brilliant that he fell at His feet as dead. This last book of Scripture gives us the full blaze of the majesty of His Person and the greatness of His power. The marvel of grace is that if this Beloved is ours and we are His, then we shall share eternal bliss with Him.

THE LATTICE OF OUR CIRCUMSTANCES

The clouds often surrounding our life are but the hiding of our precious Lord behind the lattice. But behind a frowning providence He hides a smiling face. Our Beloved is ever near, and is most near when He seems so far off. Was this not the experience of Job when he said,

> *Behold, I go forward, but He is not there; and backward, but I cannot perceive Him: on the left hand, where He does work, but I cannot behold Him: He hides Himself on the right hand, that I cannot see Him: but He knows the way*

---

34. Horatius Bonar, "This is the Hour of Banquet and of Song," 1855.

that I take: when He has tried me, I shall come forth as
gold. (Job 23:8–10)

What if His form we cannot see? We feel and know that He is near, behind the wall of adversity, the window of sorrow, and the lattice of need. His is a blessed concealment, as Isaiah experienced when he prayed, *"Verily You are a God that hides Yourself"* (Isaiah 45:15).

THE LATTICE OF OUR WITNESS

In the Old Testament the Lord often drew near to men as a wayfaring man, assuming a human form, or appearing in angelic guise. Thus He talked to Joshua, to Abraham, to the wife of Manoah, and to others, and the particular form He adopted was for the time being just a lattice.

Now He waits to make our lives the lattice through which He can display His holiness. Is He, as our Beloved, manifesting Himself as fully as He desires to others through our witness, or are we blocking the revelation? May we realize that He waits to reveal His beauty through the lattice work of our daily life, thereby shedding the fragrance of His presence all around!

As the hymnist, James Mountain, so aptly puts it:

Then with the gift of holiness within us:
We are not less human, but made more divine:
Our lives replete with Heaven's supernal beauty,
Ever declare that beauty, Lord, is Thine.[35]

---

35. James Mountain, "The Fruit of the Spirit," circa 1900.

Chapter 9

THE LITTLE FOXES

*T*he Shulamite sings in her ditty about the foxes ruining the vineyards when laden with fruit. *"Take us the foxes, the little foxes, that spoil the vines: for our vines have tender grapes"* (Song of Solomon 2:15). Ellicott suggests this line may be from a verse of a familiar country song, seeing the ancient poets were fond of addressing love songs to mischievous and troublesome creatures.

THE MEANING OF "FOX"

The word *fox* is from an original term meaning, "to hollow out," referring to the burrow or hole the fox makes and lives in. Biblical references to these omnivorous creatures give not only their natural characteristics but also their symbolic significance. David wrote, *"Those that seek my soul, to destroy it, shall go into the lower parts of the earth. They shall fall by the sword: they shall be a portion for foxes"* (Psalm 63:9–10). Their destructive, devouring

It only takes
one sin
to make a sinner,
and the little fox we
play with today will
turn and attack
us when
fully developed.

power calls to mind Peter's cameo of the devil as one "going about to devour." Solomon describes the devastating power of the little foxes spoiling the vines with their tender grapes. Israelite vinedressers dreaded a plague of foxes which, through their cunning, could cause them disastrous losses. The Hebrews looked upon the vine as the noblest, most fruitful and beautiful of plants and would surround it with thick hedges or mud walls to protect its fruit from thieves. But the worst robber was the fox, because it could not be seen. While the owner watched that no one climbed over the mud wall to steal the fruit, the thievish fox would dig a hole under the wall and soon devour the grapes.

To sacred writers, the vine was a favorite illustration of Israel, of our Lord, and also of crafty men. (See Psalm 80:8; Hosea 10:1; John 15:1; Matthew 26:29; Revelation 14:19.) John the Baptist, at the cost of his life, did not spare the fox-like Herod. (See Mark 6:20; Luke 13:32.) It is generally assumed that the *vineyard* can represent life in its entirety; the *grapes*, the fruit of the Holy Spirit; the *foxes*, the sins destroying such fruit.

The Parent Foxes

The parent foxes symbolize the full grown or more conspicuous sins spoiling the life. When David cried, *"My sin is ever before me"* (Psalm 51:3), he was referring to the great and glaring sin of adultery that resulted in deceit and murder. Doubtless we shrink at committing a sin of this magnitude. But the little foxes are easier to ignore.

The Little Foxes

The little foxes do more damage to the vines because they are small and not easily seen. When we speak of little sins, we mean insignificant offenses. Solomon reminds us that a little folly can be disastrous to one who has a reputation for wisdom and honor. (See Ecclesiastes 10:1.) Little sins can become parents of the greatest. (See 1 Corinthians 5:6.) Did not James say that he who offends in one point is guilty of all? (See James 2:10.)

THE DANGER OF THE LITTLE FOXES

It only takes one sin to make a sinner, and the little fox we play with today will turn and attack us when fully developed. A small beginning can end in a tragic disaster. Solomon knew from experience how little foxes could bore their way into the vineyard of a life and spoil its fruit. How nobly he commenced his reign, how tragically he ended it!

Because little foxes can work irreparable havoc, may we take the salutary admonition of the Shulamite to heart. These small creatures can symbolize:

- Little compromises with the world. We are not as strict as we ought to be regarding complete separation from all detrimental worldly pursuits.

- Little strokes of policy or wire-pulling deemed necessary if one is to get on in church or business.

- Little acts of disobedience in the matter of fleshly indulgences such as eating, drinking, and smoking.

- Little practices in money matters. How guilty we are of the misuse of money! How unwilling are we to loosen our purse-strings on behalf of the needy and extend Christ's cause among the lost? Perhaps we are as lax regarding our obligation to pay our debts?

94

+ Little indulgences in self-pleasure such as unnecessary attention to dress or facial beauty.

God's business and our own requires constant watch lest we fail to discern and obey the still small voice in things we call trifles. May we be preserved from the dead and unlovely flies in the perfume of our character. We harbor these little foxes, a most prolific brood, to the loss of our spiritual influence for our Lord who is without spot or wrinkle.

Have we faults of temper that we call trivial but which mar our testimony and diminish our power for God? Have we an impatient spirit, demanding that everything be done in a hurry? We do not possess our souls in patience. Have we the critical spirit, quick to blame and unready to praise? Have we the discontented spirit that nothing pleases, whether it is food, the weather, or our circumstances?

95

Have we the selfish, self-pleasing frame of mind or the anxious mind or worrying care? Foxes of distrust must be drastically dealt with. Have we a proud heart, too big to learn, too self-important, destitute of humility? Have we a bitter tongue or a gossiping one, prone to engage in the disparagement of others, or a boastful tongue, praising personal qualities and achievements?

As little foxes spoil the grapes, so these so-called little sins work tremendous havoc in at least three ways:

+ In our *upward* life—our communion with our holy Lord in the heavenlies.

+ In our *inward* life—our fence is the Lord, and our serenity and rest.

If the
Lord fills
our entire being,
there will be **no room**
for foxes, large or
small, to **hide.**

+ In our *outward* life—our service for the Lord, and loss of spiritual power.

One of the more poignant passages in the Gospels is when Jesus says, *"Foxes have holes, and birds of the air have nests; but the Son of man has not where to lay His head"* (Luke 9:58).

If the Lord fills our entire being, there will be no room for foxes, large or small, to hide. Foxes hate the light and work at night, attacking the vineyard as the keeper sleeps. How constantly we must watch and pray lest the foxes of sin tunnel in the dark. Alexander Smellie's illustration is appropriate:

> In the heart of the forest a great tree falls with a sudden crash. What has occasioned its downfall? Not the merciless stroke of the lightning. Not the swift edge of the workman's axe. No, but some tiny insect which, bit by bit and hour after hour, has eaten away the living core out of the tree.[36]

Should we not beware of those infinitesimal, invisible, and insidious insects bent on destroying the trees of the Lord that should be full of sap and flourishing? Solomon reminds us of the way we can be delivered from the subtle, undetected movements of the destructive forces of evil: *"Take us the foxes"* (Song of Solomon 2:15). *"Take"* means *catch* or *destroy*. These must be caught *in time* before the grapes are ripe. *"Us"* speaks of partnership. The vineyard in the narration was the mutual possession

---

36. Alexander Smellie, *On the Secret Place* (London: Andrew Melrose, 1907), 73.

Our glorious Victor is the One who is more than able to keep our vineyard of life and service.

of the Shulamite and her beloved, and our protection against satanic foxes is a matter of mutual concern and responsibility.

THE HUMAN PART

Fox-hunting is condemned by many animal lovers because it results not only in a maddened animal but also a cruel death. But when the little foxes spoil the grapes of holiness, it is not cruel to be in earnest about cleansing ourselves from all filthiness of the flesh. We must drag the foxes out of their holes with the light of His countenance. In cold countries the fur of the fox turns white as snow, which is a remarkable plan of nature for protection. Our protection, however, against the deceit and camouflage is in the confession of our sins to the Lord who alone is able to protect and preserve us.

99

THE DIVINE PART

We cannot perfect holiness in the fear of the Lord apart from Him who has been made unto us sanctification. All Persons of the Trinity are united in the safety of the grapes and in the vineyard of life and service.

The Father is the Husbandman;
The Believer is the Vineyard;
The Son is the Purchaser of the Vineyard;
The Holy Spirit is the Vine-dresser;
The Grapes represent the fruit of the Spirit.

The story is told of a fox taken in a trap that bit its leg off and thus escaped although badly crippled. It is folly to try to slay those evil forces seeking to entrap us ourselves. Our glorious

Victor, Prince Divine, is the One who is more than able to keep our vineyard clear of destructive foxes, when we see we cannot do it alone.

As Ralph Erskine expresses it:

The foxes' tender brood destroy,
   Their cries for pity hush;
Else they thy buds of grace and joy
   Thy tender branch will crush.

Chapter 10

THE GRACEFUL GAZELLE

King Solomon, chief of all naturalists, knew about the distinctive features of the animals he used metaphorically in his notable love idyll to symbolize the Savior and His love for His own and of their love for Him.

Solomon apparently had a peculiar interest in roes, seen in that he makes this familiar and graceful antelope the illustration of the bride's appreciation of the bridegroom, and vice versa. (See Song of Solomon 2:7, 9; 3:5, 17; 4:5; 7:3; 8:14.)

Under the Hebrew word for roe, *isebi* or *isebiyah*, we have a large variety of animals. There is the hart, roe, hind, or roebuck, occurring as a metaphor or representing animals lawful as food and which therefore belonged to the true ruminants, fit to eat at Solomon's table. (See 1 Kings 4:23.) All have similar habits and characteristics, being varieties of *gazella dorcas*. The hart is the male member of the family and the hind, the female. The name *gazelle* is used for *roe* in the American Standard Version. Its attractive features include its acknowledged beauty, its being without gall, its being good for food, and its remarkable agility.

ACKNOWLEDGED BEAUTY

The poet/king describes it as the *"pleasant roe"* (Proverbs 5:19). It is delightful to watch a roe running, its self-dignity being evident. Its large, soft, liquid eyes were often used by Eastern poets to describe eyes of instant and impressive appeal. Thomas Moore (1779–1852) wrote: "I never nursed a dear gazelle, to glad me with its soft black eye," a couplet Charles Dickens then used for one of his characters.

Lord Byron wrote, "Her eye's dark charm 'twere vain to tell: / But gaze on that of the gazelle, / It will assist thy fancy well." Yet another could write of "cruel gazelles, with graceful gait and liquid eye."

We have an allusion to its beauty in the well-known name *Tabitha* which in the Hebrew means "the Gazelle." (See Acts 9:36.) Its Greek name, Dorcas, implies the lovely character of the woman who was full of good works and deeds.

The psalmist often refers to the beauty of the Lord. No halo that artists cast around Him can impart the glow of grace and warmth of love that drew sad and hungry hearts to Him. Think of those soft eyes of His, liquid with tears, as He weeps over a lost city! How we need Spirit-anointed eyes to discern His beauty!

WITHOUT GALL

Naturalists are agreed that the gazelle does not have a gall-bladder, the organ that secretes bile. The Bible associates *gall* with *bitterness*. Peter told Simon the Sorcerer that he was in *"the gall of bitterness,"* that is, in a state of extreme hostility to God (Acts 8:23). It is the absence of gall that makes the gazelle sweet, docile, pleasant, and attractive. A common operation today is the removal of the gall bladder. Many of us could do with a similar operation in the spiritual realm, for we can be very bitter in our treatment of others.

Do we not have an appealing symbol in this feature of Jesus who bore no envy, revenge, or spirit of bitterness over the harsh treatment accorded Him? When He was dying, grace was His to pray for the forgiveness of those who murdered Him. May we be like Naphtali, "a graceful hind," or one let loose giving words of pleasure (see Genesis 49:21). Grace and gall do not go together, beauty and bitterness do not agree.

103

GOOD FOR FOOD

Reckoned among the clean animals and therefore fit to be eaten, such a creature is almost too noble to be slain and consumed as food. (See Deuteronomy 12:15, 21; 14:5.) The same permission is repeated but with the proviso that its blood shall be poured out on the earth like water. (See Deuteronomy 15:22–23.)

In his volume on *Bible Animals*, J. G. Wood says of the flesh of the gazelle, or roe, that it is still considered "a great dainty, although it is not agreeable to European taste, being hard, and without flavor." The gazelle was held in high esteem among the Jews as a delicacy seen in the rich repast provided for Solomon's table. (See 1 Kings 4:23.) But while lawful for food, it was never to be used as a sacrifice.

Through
His sacrifice
we have life and
unfailing
nourishment.

How different for Jesus. Yet without the shedding of His blood, He could not have become our bread. His blood, like that of the gazelle, was poured out as water on the earth, and through His sacrifice we have life and unfailing nourishment.

"*Thy two breasts are like two fawns that are twins of a roe*" (Song of Solomon 4:5; 7:3 ASV). The bride had praised her beloved as being "like a gazelle"; now his reciprocated praise is in this delicate reference to the beauty of the female body. In Scripture "*breasts*" represent life-giving properties. In his prophetic benediction given to his sons, Jacob prayed that the "*blessings of the breasts*" might be theirs (Genesis 49:25). Isaiah, in his praise of Jerusalem, called upon all that loved her to "*be satisfied with the breasts of her consolations; that you may milk out, and be delighted with the abundance of her glory*" (Isaiah 66:11).

105

In the divine name, *El Shaddai*, the almighty One who compels nature to act contrary to itself, the single term *Shaddai* comes from the root *Shad*, which means "breast" and is the Hebrew word Jacob used in the "*blessings of the breasts.*" Such a delicate yet precious metaphor presents God as One who nourishes, supplies, and satisfies the soul, as the milk of a mother's breasts gives life to her babe. Wrote Dr. G. Campbell Morgan, "To gather sustenance and consolation from the bosom of God is to be made strong for all the pilgrimage." *Shaddai* reminds us of God as "The Breasted One," the Provider of blessings, spiritual or temporal. Andrew Jukes summarizes this in his *Genesis*:

God almightiness is of the breast, that is, of bountiful, self-sacrificing love, giving and pouring itself out for others. Therefore, He can quiet the restless, as the breast quiets the child; therefore He can nourish and strengthen as the breast nourishes; therefore He can attract, as the breast attracts, when we are in peril of falling from Him.

As the bride is a symbol of the church, the church's two breasts are *life* and *witness*, so effective to quiet, refresh, nourish, and satisfy those crying, restless souls around her. There are other features of the graceful gazelle such as its love of music, keen faculties, affection, aversion to serpents, but we conclude with the mutual way in which the beloved and his spouse extol the animal for its agility.

REMARKABLE AGILITY

106

The alacrity and speed of the gazelle is among its most noticeable qualities. Thomson in *The Land and the Book* says, "I have often stopped to admire the grace, the ease, the fearless security with which these pretty animals bound along the high places of the mountains."

Wood, in his valuable work on *Bible Animals*, observes, "So fleet is the gazelle, or roe, that it seems to fly over ground as if propelled by volition alone, and its light, agile frame is so enduring, that a fair chase has hardly any prospect of success."

It is said of the Gadites, faithful followers of David, that because of the swift movements in war they *"were as swift as the roes [gazelles] upon the mountains"* (1 Chronicles 12:8). The ability of the gazelle to leap and skip over hills and its gracefulness of action in motion are features often alluded to in the Bible. (See Psalm 18:33; Habakkuk 3:19.) Asahel, brother of Joab, has the reputation of being *"as light of foot as a wild roe"* (2 Samuel 2:18).

The wisdom of the Creator is seen in the way He has given to man, animal, and bird the kind of feet each requires to walk upon, or use.

Man's foot, for example, is very strong, very elastic, with its twenty-six delicate bones held together by bands of great strength. It is also helped by its graceful arch.

The elephant's foot is so formed to bear the strain of its massive body and low-set knees.

The camel's foot is made of two toes connected by a broad elastic pad on which the foot rests, and which bear up the animal as it carries its load over the shifting sands of the desert.

The duck's foot is short and webbed and therefore properly suitable for wading in shallow water. This provision also enables it to swim with swiftness and gracefulness over the lake. Other birds' feet are arranged into classes according to the kind of feet they have and the uses to which they put them.

A gazelle's feet have solid hoofs, as hard as steel, rough underneath, and when walking on a flat surface, they are capable of being spread over. Because of the structure of its feet, it is able to balance itself on the smallest foothold as it scales almost perpendicular rocks. With its feet it can lay hold of the slightest projection and, when pursued, can skip over hills and valleys with astounding speed coupled with beauty and grace. So we can readily grasp the often repeated application of their feet in Scripture.

The Holy Spirit can similarly supply us with strong and nimble feet and shoes that will never wear out to travel over the hard road ahead. The Lord is able to grant us the unobstructed

With what
alacrity and swiftness
did our
Beloved accomplish
the will of His Father,
and how speedily
as He came
leaping over
the mountains to
reconcile man to God.

movement and power to advance with firm, strong, unswerving steps. Paul would have us *"seek those things...above"* (Colossians 3:1); may our feet be strong to leap over the walls of sin and self and doubt and take us up from the vile flats to the alpine heights of Christian blessedness and victory.

> He to thy tardy feet still lend
> The swiftness of the roe:
> Till, raised on high, I safely dwell
> Beyond the reach of woe.[37]

Our divine Captain expects all of us as His soldiers to *"run, and not be weary"* (Isaiah 40:31), swift in fleeing from evil to Himself and just as speedy to reach the lost all around us.

> Take my feet and let them be
> Swift and beautiful for Thee.[38]

With what alacrity and swiftness did our Beloved accomplish the will of His Father, and how speedily as He came leaping over the mountains to reconcile man to God. None is so swift as He in the relief of suffering saints. The gazelle fights fiercely for its female; Jesus also is engaged in sharp conflict with the old Serpent over those who form His bride.

> The Voice of my Beloved sounds,
> Over the rocks and rising grounds:
> O'er hills of guilt and sear of grief
> He leaps, He flies to my relief.[39]

---

37. John Logan.
38. Frances Ridley Havergal, "Take My Life, and Let It Be," 1874.
39. Rev. Isaac Watts, "Hymn 69," 1806.

The final word of the Song comes from the bride, inviting the bridegroom to flee to her side, a slightly altered repetition of her previous refrain: *"Make haste, my beloved, and be you like to a roe or to a young hart upon the mountains of spices"* (Song of Solomon 8:14). Her intense love discerns the approach of the bridegroom afar off. This is reminiscent of Tennyson's lines in *Fatima*, "Before he mounts the hill, I know / He cometh quickly."

Thus, as Ellicott comments, "The poem ends with two short verses that compress into them all that has been over and over again related under different figures: the wooing and wedding of two happy souls."

How symbolic this is of the second coming of our heavenly Bridegroom who promises His bride, *"I will come again, and receive you to Myself"* (John 14:3), and of the bride's heart-felt prayer, *"Even so, come, Lord Jesus"* (Revelation 22:20). Before long, He will come leaping over all the immensities of space, and in a moment, in the twinkling of an eye, gather His redeemed around upon the mountain of spices. The somewhat abrupt, unsatisfied close of the Song with the yearning prayer of the bride for the visible coming of her beloved indicates that their final union is still future. Is this not so with all who cry, "Come, quickly, Lord Jesus!"? (See Revelation 22:7.) Presently the Beloved is ours, and we are His; the marriage of the Lamb is still future, and we are to await it with eagerness. (See 1 Thessalonians 1:10; Titus 2:13; 2 Peter 3:12; Revelation 19:7–9.)

Hark what a sound, and too divine for hearing,
  Stirs on earth and trembles in the air:
Is it the thunder of the Lord's appearing?

Is it the music of His people's prayer?
Surely He cometh, and a thousand voices
   Shout to the saints, and to the deaf and dumb:
Surely He cometh, and the earth rejoices,
   Glad in His coming Who hath sworn: I come![40]

111

40. F. W. H. Myers, "Hark What a Sound," 1867.

Chapter 11

EXPRESSIONS OF MUTUAL LOVE

To all who have an interest in poetry, the paeans of love sung one to another in Solomon's Song are unsurpassable. The voices of the beloved and his maiden, as they speak of one another and to one another, are vibrant with feeling, declaring a mutual, indissoluble love union. The term *"beloved"* occurs twenty-seven times in its eight chapters; the Septuagint uses *"kinsman,"* meaning, "one near to redeem." Our heavenly Beloved indeed!

The three related passages we will consider in this passage are: *"My beloved is mine, and I am his"* (Song of Solomon 2:16). *"I am my beloved's, and my beloved is mine"* (6:3). *"I am my beloved's, and his desire is toward me"* (7:10).

In the first passage (2:16), the Shulamite's love for her beloved is a pledge that she is his, and this consoled her in his absence. With the assurance of their unchangeable, mutual devotion, she bids her lover, pasturing his flock in the fields bright with lilies, to hasten to her side. The two lovers Solomon wove his Song around were pure in heart and life and were as one.

Jesus declared, *"He that loves Me shall be loved of My Father, and I will love him"* (John 14:21). As believers, we are partakers of Christ, taken not only into covenant but into union and communion with Him.

In the second passage (6:13), the order of clauses is reversed; the bride now resting more on being the bridegroom's and not on his being hers. In her loneliness she grounds her conviction on his love toward her more than on hers toward him. On a higher level, Moses wrote that God *"loved the people; all His saints are in [His] hand"* (Deuteronomy 33:3). The emphasis here is on the divine side of love, as it is throughout Scripture.

113

The third passage (7:10) indicates the maiden's strong assurance that her beloved had a desire ever to be near her, which intensified hers ever to be at his side. This is also true of Christ and His own, with whom He desired to eat the Passover. (See Luke 22:15–16; 1 John 4:16.)

Matthew Henry has the apt comment:

Christ's desire is strong towards His chosen remnant, when He came from heaven to earth to seek and save them. This is a comfort to believers that, whosoever slights them, Christ has a desire towards them, and such a desire as will again bring Him from heaven to earth to receive them to Himself.

All three passages indicate the deepening love and appreciation of lovers one toward the other and symbolize the progress of faith and growing spiritual comprehension on the part of the believer. *"Let us go on"* (Hebrews 6:1) is the motto the writer of the letter to the Hebrews would have us adopt. The first verse of Theodore Monod's heart-searching hymn "O the Bitter Shame and Sorrow" ends, "All of self, and none of Thee," which refers to life before conversion, when the kiss of reconciliation is received. The next three verses can express the marked stages of the Shulamite's appreciation of, and association with, her beloved.

"Some of self, and some of Thee!" is her attitude in 2:16.

"Less of self, and more of Thee!" is her voice in 6:3.

"None of self, and all of Thee!" is her submission in 7:10.

114   Similarly, there are three forcible statements in the Word showing the saint's progress in his relationship to the heavenly Bridegroom.

"They feared the LORD, *and served their own gods"* (2 Kings 17:33).

"He must increase, but I must decrease" (John 3:30).

"I am crucified with Christ: nevertheless I live; yet not I, but Christ lives in me" (Galatians 2:20).

Let us look a little more deeply into the expressions of mutual love between the maiden and her beloved.

MY BELOVED IS MINE AND I AM HIS

The original of the maiden's first expression reads, "My beloved is for me, and I am for him" (see 2:16). This can represent the starting point of Christian experience when the believer is taken up with the *possession of Christ* and thinks of Him as their own. "*I...entered into a covenant with you, says the Lord God, and you became Mine*" (Ezekiel 16:8).

The maiden's first expression demonstrates both *faith* and *consecration*.

Faith: "My beloved is mine"

This faith can be seen in a threefold dimension: as a gift of the Father (see John 3:16; 1 John 4:10); as Christ's own personal gift (see Ephesians 5:25); and as communicated to us by the Holy Spirit (see Ephesians 3:17).

Ignatius, the notable early father, called himself a "God-bearer." Asked what he meant by it, friends received his reply, "I carry God about with me: our bodies are the temples of the Holy Ghost." Such is the faith that can sing in an unpresumptuous vein, "O, I am my Beloved's and my Beloved's mine." Note the Shulamite used an emphatic "*Is* mine," in other words, "is my present possession." So the Christian can say:

Blessed assurance! Jesus *is* mine;
Oh, what a foretaste of glory divine![41]

The Beloved is mine, *mine* in every way: mine to deliver me from the penalty and power of sin, mine to clothe with the righteousness of God, mine to dwell in my heart by faith, mine through all the vicissitudes of life, mine through death's dark vale, mine in heavenly glory forevermore, and mine to speak to, look to, and give my cares to.

---

41. Fanny Crosby, "Blessed Assurance," 1873, emphasis added.

He desires me, cares for me, loves me, lives in me, and centers His attention and action upon me.

Consecration: "I am his"

The Shulamite was called a *dove* in the clefts of the rock, but her beloved drew her out and made her his own. Through a covenant relationship, we are the Lord's, and therefore the responsibility of our life is His. We are His by creation, redemption, conquest of the Holy Spirit, and by our own free consent. On our Lord's part, He went into battle against Satan and our own stubborn will, and won. Thus we are reckoned as a *possession in Christ*. May we not rest here, though, but travel on to experience His grace and power in a fuller measure.

> Have you on the Lord believed?
>   Still there's more to follow.
> Of His grace have you received?
>   Still there's more to follow.[42]

I AM MY BELOVED'S, AND MY BELOVED IS MINE

The Shulamite is still speaking and is heard expressing her jealousy for her beloved. First, the beloved came first! Now the beginning is "*I am my beloved's*," indicating complete ownership and allegiance to him.

Spiritually, the changed language suggests an advance in Christian experience, a deepening intimacy, the realization of a personal Pentecost founded on Calvary. His ownership of us now takes the first place in our life: what *He* has, not merely what *I* have. As we grow in grace, Christ's ownership of us has the preeminence; and His interests, not ours, come first. If we are for our Beloved and He is for us, there is no room ever to

42. Philip P. Bliss, "Have You on the Lord Believed?" 1873.

117

question either His direct or permissive will. Can we confess that ours is an unbroken heart occupation with Jesus? W. J. Govan has poetically expressed it:

> He makes His palace in my soul,
>   He brings my spirit nigh:
> Within my heart, 'neath His control
>   I dwell, my Lord and I.

If, in deep experiences of life, it seems as if the Beloved's face is hidden from us and we lack the full assurance of His unchanging love and presence, then we must still trust and adhere to Him who can never make a mistake in the ordering of your life and mine. Matthew Henry's comment on this verse is, "Though I have not the sensible consolation I used to have, yet I will cleave to this, Christ is mine and I am His."

I AM MY BELOVED'S, AND HIS DESIRE IS TOWARD ME

No other beloved had any charm for the maiden. (See Song of Solomon 5:9.) The *mine* is dropped as she exultingly exclaims, "I belong to my beloved alone, and he, on his part, longs after me only." Such a verse implies further progress to a still closer intimacy, for she is joyfully aware of his affections for her and no one else. The progress of those who follow on to know the Lord, namely possession *for Christ*, is similarly: what I have in Him (2:16); what He has in me (6:3); what He wants from me (7:10).

To be His involves all we have and are. *Mine* is eliminated; self-glory, self-interest, self-reliance vanish. "None of self, but all of Thee." The more we acquiesce to His desire toward us, the clearer we perceive all He requires of us and the more precious

His thoughts of us become. (See Psalm 139:17.) So we know that as our King He greatly desires our beauty. (See Psalm 45:11.)

Think of it! He desires me, cares for me, loves me, lives in me, and centers His attention and action upon *me*. What a glorious life to live!

Chapter 12:

STRIKING PORTRAITS OF THE BRIDE

One of the most conservative theologians of a past generation was the renowned Israeli scholar, Godet, whose interpretation of The Song of Solomon is that Solomon represents the earthly kingship Israel experienced; that the Shulamite typifies Israel after the gift of the Spirit; the daughters of Jerusalem represent Israel after the flesh; the Shepherd-Lover, the Lord God. His book teaches the transfer of Israel from a theocracy to a monarchy; her scattering among the nations; her present plight; her regathering by the absent Lover when they meet under the apple tree as the millennium dawns.

Thus, all the figures drawn from nature depict the Land of Promise, center of the habitable world and chosen because of its great beauty and fruitfulness. Godet emphasizes that this land became the home of the Jews by divine arrangement: This central spot has already been the scene of events far surpassing all others in their importance and results; and it shall yet be the scene of events, for which the heavens and the earth are waiting, and to which all Scripture points.

Through her failure to obey God, Israel has found Jerusalem a troubled place in which to live, yet it will become the glory of all nations, as Moses prophesied. (See Deuteronomy 8:7–10; 34:1–8.) In the future, the land is to become exceedingly fertile. If we follow Godet's exposition, Solomon, a natural figure, describes the land God gave to His people and His undying love for them and their future, undivided love for Him.

Solomon also gives us three striking portraits of the bride in the Song: *"A garden enclosed"* is my sister, my spouse; *"a spring shut up,"* a *"fountain sealed"* (4:12). Let us look into the figurative pictures given to us from this description of the bride.

121

THREE PICTURES OF OLD TESTAMENT TEACHING

In his lavish praise of the charm and fragrance of his bride, the beloved used three metaphors describing a pure, chaste wife barred to all others, and one who was his very own to whom he and he alone had delight. So she invites the beloved to come into his garden and satisfy his heart with all she has. (See Song of Solomon 4:16.) Let us look now at their metaphorical and spiritual application.

The Garden Enclosed

The Bible, as a whole, contains a progressive revelation, the Old Testament being only a partial revelation. *"Enclosed"* means "barred" in Hebrew.

There is the barring of Adam from the garden of Eden because of his sin. (See Genesis 3:22–24.) Direct access to God

No longer is the spring shut up, for Christ provided us with a well of water, overflowing.

was made impossible by the flaming sword, and approach to God was then through prophets and priests.

But the commendation of the Shulamite by her beloved, *"Thou art a fountain of gardens"* (4:15 ASV), brings in the New Testament truth that now, through grace, there is nothing to bar the believer from coming boldly to the throne of grace. No longer is the spring shut up, for Christ provided us with a well of water, overflowing. (See John 4:14.) The fullest access will come when all bars are removed and this garden is open for the health of all nations. (See Revelation 22:1–5.) Christ was a garden enclosed in heaven, but in His incarnation, He leaped the barrier to succeed where the first Adam had failed. The gardens of Gethsemane and Calvary brought Him much sorrow and anguish, but He rose from His garden tomb, providing direct access to God through His redemptive sacrifice.

123

In Old Testament days, the word of God was rare, or precious, and there was no frequent, or widely spread, vision. (See 1 Samuel 3:1.) The revelation that was given was possessed by one nation only; Israel herself became a garden enclosed by the partition of the ceremonial law, designed especially for her. Through Christ this wall was removed. In Him there is neither Jew nor Gentile, only sinners saved by His matchless grace, through which we now have a complete revelation. Paul was privileged to reveal the fullness of God's provision and to declare past mysteries. As those who have the complete Bible, we must guard against disobedience to what it reveals. Lack of spiritual intuition can keep the Word as a garden enclosed, a garden barred. The Holy Spirit, who inspired holy men of old to prepare the sacred garden of Scripture for us, is with us to show us its fruits and flowers. As we enter this garden, having no barriers, our prayer and purpose must be Elihu's: *"That which I see not teach You me: if I have done iniquity, I will do no more"* (Job 34:32).

A Spring Shut Up

As the garden enclosed beautifully describes the divine protection of God's ancient people, and also of the church set apart for the Lord himself (see Psalm 4:3; Isaiah 5:1–2; Matthew 16:18), so *"the spring shut up"* is latent with spiritual truth. Of old, springs and fountains were sealed to save them from being polluted or muddied. The beloved testified to the pure state of his spouse when he called her his *"undefiled"*, and here accentuates her purity as a sealed spring. Open springs often pass away (see John 4:13; 2 Peter 2:17), but the spring the bride represents ever remains, for its source is in heaven (see Revelation 22:17). To drink from springs of the world is folly. (See Proverbs 5:15–16.)

John uses the phrase, *"the Spirit and the bride"* (Revelation 22:17). Water is one of the symbols used of the Spirit, and as He gave the bride, the church, her birthday at Pentecost, He is her never-failing spring. In the Old Testament, He was more or less sealed, the Holy Spirit only coming upon individuals for the accomplishment of a particular mission and leaving them when their task was completed. (See Psalm 51:11.)

In the New Testament the Holy Spirit is a well of living water and, as a Person, abides with those He is within. (See John 7:37–39.) The story of Acts, and of the church down the ages, is that wherever He flows, there is life. Although we have been sealed with the Spirit, there is no sealing of His power in our witness. (See Ephesians 4:30; 2 Timothy 2:19.)

THREE PICTURES OF THE BELIEVER'S SECURITY

The illustration the beloved used of his lover can be applied to the believer's present and eternal security. The church is aptly compared to a garden with its spring and fountain because she has been set apart for God and walks in Him unseen. The church is composed of His hidden ones, enclosed for safety and protected from surrounding powers of darkness.

A Garden Barred

The believer is like a garden whose gardener is the Lord, ever active, cultivating the believer to bear the fruit of holiness. Sealed with His seal, the follower is closed against all pollutants and bears fragrant fruit for Him alone. The child of God is also enclosed for secrecy. He is God's private possession, is not for strangers, and seeks to dwell in the secret place.

Shut up to Christ also implies safety. Gardens in the East were always enclosed with a fence of reeds, strong hedges, or a stone wall. "*Have not You made an hedge* [around] *him?*" (Job 1:10; see also Isaiah 5:1–7). Is not the Lord round about us as the mountains are round about Jerusalem? Isaac Watts poetically describes this in the stanza:

> We are a garden walled around,
> Chosen and made peculiar ground;
> A little spot enclosed by Grace,
> Out of the world's wide wilderness.

A Spring Shut Up

Behind the metaphors Solomon put into the mouth of the beloved is the seclusion of women in the East and their chastity.

125

The believer is like a garden whose gardener is the Lord, ever active, cultivating the believer to bear the fruit of holiness.

Tradition has it that Solomon shut up his springs and sealed the door with his own signet to preserve their fresh, pure water for his own drinking.

While our love no longer flows out for the sins and pleasure of the world, but flows inward to Jesus, is His love streaming out through us to those who are dead to sin, or are we as a spring shut up?

A Fountain Sealed

Sealed in, and by, the Holy Spirit, we have no fear of pollution. We are also secure until the day of our redemption, or entrance into glory. (See Ephesians 4:30.) He is still the Fountain sealed for the ungodly, but for us, He is the Fountain opened, when there flowed from His gashed side blood and water. Now we have the prospect of eternal security, bliss, and provision in the garden of paradise from which we shall never be cast out. Nothing unclean can enter the garden with its perennial fountains for our everlasting refreshment. (See Revelation 21:27.) Our obligation now is to strive after the life which is like a watered garden, full of fragrance rare, not disappointing the Lord because of the lack of fruit. (See Luke 13:6.) If fruitlessness is ours, we must expect the wind to blow upon our garden and banish the barrenness and dryness so that our Beloved can cut of His precious fruits.

For our daily life and living, the *garden* implies fruitfulness; the *spring*, freshness; the *fountain*, fullness.

> Happy enclosure! Where the piercing gale
> Nips but the budding weeds, while, left secure.
> The cultured plants are refuged from all ill
> To flourish in the soft succeeding calm.

Chapter 13

A GARDEN OF SPICES

Awake, O north wind; and come, you south; blow upon my garden, that the spices thereof may flow out. Let my beloved come into his garden, and eat his pleasant fruits.
—Song of Solomon 4:16

AN EPITOME OF THE NEW TESTAMENT

In the three clauses above we have a bird's eye view of the three sections of the New Testament.

The North Wind and the Gospels

The Gospels cover the historical: the life, death, and resurrection of Jesus, and His preparation for the church.

The call in the first clause, *"Awake, O north wind; and come, you south,"* can express the work of the Holy Spirit, who was to come with "*a sound from heaven as of a rushing mighty wind*" (Acts 2:2). The world awaited the Breath of God; in like manner we have the call of Jesus for the Father to send the Spirit whom He had likened unto "*wind*" (John 3:8; see also 14:16). Jesus declared it was expedient for Him to leave the earth so that the invisible Spirit might come. (See John 16:7.)

John Keble expresses the disciples' puzzlement over this: "My Savior, can it ever be / That I should gain by losing Thee?"

When here in the flesh, Jesus could only be in one place at a time, but now His presence can be realized by the Spirit wherever a saint is found. The spices of the garden—the life, death, and resurrection of Jesus—need the Holy Spirit to diffuse them today, to lead us into the truth concerning them.

Our Lord's teaching in John 16 on the Spirit's ministry is fragrantly profound. "With a few great strokes He depicts all and every part of the ministry of the Holy Spirit in the world, and His operation with reference to individuals as well as the mass, on believers and unbelievers alike."[43]

At Calvary the Holy Spirit was the "*north wind*," for it was through the eternal Spirit that Jesus offered Himself up to God. At Pentecost He is seen as the creative, exhilarating "*south wind*." As the north wind He reproves and convicts the sinner. (See John 16:8.) As the south wind He is the Comforter, Teacher, Indweller. (See John 14:16–18; 16:13–15.) If Jesus recognized the necessity of the Holy Spirit to make His work effectual, how much the more is our utter dependence upon Him for life and witness?

---

43. Robert Jamieson, *Commentary*, vol. 1 (Hartford, CT: S. S. Scranton & Co., 1871).

The South Wind and the Acts and Epistles

The Acts and Epistles cover the doctrinal with their record of the institution, development, and instruction of the church.

In Acts we have the formation of the church by the Holy Spirit, while in the Epistles we have the church built up and taught all facets of Christian truth. Thus the second clause, *"Blow upon my garden, that the spices thereof may flow out"* (Song of Solomon 4:16), was fulfilled. Before He left His own, Jesus commissioned them to go out into the world and preach the gospel, and the spices flowed forth as the apostles became witnesses of their glorified Beloved. (See Mark 16:15; Acts 1:8.)

Coming into the Garden and the Book of Revelation

130

Revelation contains the prophetical: Christ's letters to the church and a coverage of the consummation of all things.

The last clause of the Shulamite's plea, *"Let my beloved come into his garden, and eat his pleasant fruits"* (4:16), summarizes the Apocalypse, for its prominent message is the return of Jesus to take to himself His power to reign as King of Kings and Lord of Lords.

He Will Eat of the Pleasant Fruits of His Church

The rapture of the true church is seen in the command, *"Come up here"* (Revelation 4:1; 11:12). Then will our Redeemer be fully satisfied over His toil to bring His bride into being, and the Redeemer and the redeemed will dwell together in perfect bliss: *"Behold I and the children which God has given Me"* (Hebrews 2:13).

He Will Eat of the Pleasant Fruits of Israel

Through the winds of judgment the Jews are now scattered abroad, but they are to see Him whom they pierced reigning as their King, proudly announcing, *"Israel My glory"* (Isaiah 46:13).

He Will Eat of the Pleasant Fruits Throughout Eternity

When all of earth has been brought under the supreme control of Christ and He has delivered up the kingdom to His Father, eternal joy will be our portion. Then, as Isaac Watts has expressed it, His kingdom is to stretch from shore to shore and

> To Him shall endless prayer be made,
> And princes throng to crown His head;
> His name like sweet perfume shall rise
> With every morning sacrifice.[44]

131

A CAMEO OF THE CHRISTIAN LIFE

The symbol of the garden applied to the believer is apt and common to Scripture:

"The vineyard which Your right hand has planted" (Psalm 80:15).

"You shall be like a watered garden, and like a spring of water, whose waters fail not" (Isaiah 58:11).

"They might be called trees of righteousness, the planting of the Lord*"* (Isaiah 61:3).

The Process It Requires

"Awake, O north wind; and come, you south" (Song of Solomon 4:16). The forces of nature are the mightiest and most

---

44. Isaac Watts, "Jesus Shall Reign," 1719.

necessary factors if a natural garden is to flower and bear fruit. So also in the spiritual realm is it imperative to have the right kind of provision in the garden of heart, life, and service to yield the fruit of the Spirit. Some of these winds are the ministries of providence and the operations of the Spirit.

The Ministries of Providence

The two winds of God often awake upon our lives and blow upon our gardens, releasing the spices pleasing to our Beloved. Sorrow, affliction, adversity, crosses, and losses can come with the biting north wind. The psalmist could confess, *"It is good for me that I have been afflicted; that I might learn Your statutes"* (Psalm 119:71).

132

The south wind brings balmy air and can typify the joys, pleasures, and prosperity our life in Christ produces. Praise God, we have more of the balmy air than the biting wind! The One who owns the garden of our life knows how to carefully adjust and control the opposing winds. He will not break the bruised reed. *"He stays His rough wind in the day of the east wind"* (Isaiah 27:8). How good of God it is to place the two winds—"the airs of His love"—together. *"Behold therefore the goodness and severity of God"* (Romans 11:22).

The Operations of the Spirit

In His conversation with Nicodemus, Jesus used the symbol of the wind to describe the ministry of the Spirit in regeneration and at Pentecost. He came upon those awaiting His promised advent as the sound of a mighty rushing wind. (See John 3:8; Acts 2:2.)

As the *north* wind, He arises strongly as the Reprover of sin, convicting the sinner of his helpless condition before God.

He searches the heart, revealing where both saints and sinners fail. (See John 16:8–11.)

As the *south* wind, He comes gently as the Comforter, to cheer and gladden. In Israel the north wind is cool; the south wind, warm. After the Spirit's correction in the north wind, there comes the balmy air of surrender, and His reviving grace and power. After His operation as the north wind, purifying and quickening the soul (see Job 37:22; Proverbs 25:23) and scattering the mists of guilt, error, unbelief, and sin of the soul, the Spirit infuses us with spiritual warmth, enabling the imparted grace to exhale its fragrance (see John 14:17; 2 Corinthians 4:6).

Are these not days when the church requires the action of the Spirit as a rushing mighty wind? Do we not need Him in this way in our own hearts and in His convicting power among the great mass of godless souls in the world? Do we not long for the joy revival brings, as the self-same Spirit warms and quickens our hearts? May grace be ours to set our sails to catch the divine winds as they awake upon us!

O Spirit of Love, descend,
  Come in our midst, we pray,
And like a rushing, mighty wind
  Sweep over our souls today.[45]

The Promise It Holds

"Blow upon my garden, that the spices thereof may flow out" (4:16). To *"blow"* means to breathe upon, and this was the benediction of Jesus as He breathed upon His disciples and said,

---

45. Henrietta E. Blair, "Thy Holy Spirit, Lord, Alone," 1906.

The
arid atmosphere
all around us, and in the
regions beyond,
is in dire need of the
fragrance of our
holy witness
and the spread of
God's warm truth

"Receive you the Holy Ghost" (John 20:22). Would that He might breathe upon us and liberate imprisoned forces!

We have the gospel in its fullness, grace, and truth in our hearts; but somehow the spices are bottled up, and their fragrance is not diffused. It was only when Mary broke her box of ointment that the house was heavy with its perfume. Often in a garden, the fragrance of flowers hangs heavily above plants until the wind scatters it. Tennyson describes the effect of the gentle breeze:

> The woodbine spices are wafted abroad
> And the musk of the roses blown.

An odorless world awaits the flowing out of the spices, the grace of the Spirit, from your life and mine. The arid atmosphere all around us, and in the regions beyond, is in dire need of the fragrance of our holy witness and the spread of God's warm truth. May the winds of heaven so move upon us!

> Like a watered garden
> Full of fragrance rare,
> Lingering in Thy presence,
> Let my life appear.[46]

The Pleasure It Gives

"Let my beloved come into his garden, and eat his pleasant fruits" (4:16). The more complete our surrender to our heavenly Beloved, the less we talk of things as our own. What was once our garden is now the divine Gardener's, bought at a great price.

---

46. Emily May Grimes, "Speak, Lord in the Stillness," 1920.

Whatever we have of faith, love, humility, holiness, and truth are all His, and fruits of the Spirit. *"He came and sought fruit thereon, and found none* (Luke 13:6). May we not be barren of life and witness and so disappoint the Gardener who died to make our garden His.

Do we yearn for the full operation of the Spirit, as God's Wind, in heart and service?

> Breathe on me, Breath of God,
> Till I am wholly Thine,
> Till all this earthly part of me
> Glows with thy fire divine.[47]

Is ours the passion for a life diffusing and spreading the gospel all around? Have we the thirst for those living waters that can flow from us, if only we are fully surrendered to the Spirit's sway? Have we the longing for the return of our Beloved when He will gather all His redeemed children to Himself and through eternity eat of the precious fruit which His agony, tears, and sacrifice of Calvary produced? Our life will offer its utmost, if we can make Seagrave's poetic prayer our own:

> Wake, heavenly Wind, arise and come,
>   Blow on the drooping field:
> Our spices, then, shall breathe perfume,
>   And fragrant incense yield.[48]

47. Edwin Hatch, "Breathe on Me, Breath of God," 1878.
48. Robert Seagrave, "Now May the Spirit's Holy Fire," circa 1742.

Chapter 14

THE FISHPOOLS IN HESHBON

In the section of the Song stretching from the fourth verse of chapter six to the ninth verse of chapter seven we have the bridegroom's profound admiration for his bride. *"Return, return, O Shulamite; return, return, that we may look upon you"* (Song of Solomon 6:13).

All the parts of her form and character alike receive the beloved's commendation. *"You are **all** fair, my love"* (4:7).

In the Song of Solomon 7:4, we then have the striking figures describing three of her most notable qualities, which ancient writers saw as being typical of Israel as a nation and then of the church. In these symbols we see Israel in the heyday of her prosperity under Solomon.

"Your neck is as a tower of ivory; your eyes like the fishpools in Heshbon, by the gate of Bathrabbim: your nose is as the tower of Lebanon which looks toward Damascus" (Song of Solomon 7:4).

The upright, firm neck, not haughtily stretched, is the emblem in Scripture of a holy freedom, liberty, and independence.

Let us now look more deeply at the three qualities from the above verse.

YOUR NECK IS AS A TOWER OF IVORY

The upright, firm neck, not haughtily stretched, is the emblem in Scripture of a holy freedom, liberty, and independence. "*Ivory*," a most precious product, speaks of riches, great exaltation, and a costly possession. White, the snowy appearance of ivory, suggests purity. We can apply the symbol three ways.

Of the Shulamite herself: She carried herself with graceful independence with her lofty carriage, richness of character, and purity of heart and life.

Of Israel: When under the reigns of David and of Solomon, she had national freedom and independence, riches, honor, and glory unsurpassed in the world, but which, unfortunately, Solomon's passions and idolatry brought to an end.

139

Of the church: Does not the symbol represent the stateliness, luster, firmness, and vigor of the ambassadors of the church of God? Before mankind and the world they stand upright, firm, like a strong and stately tower, their neck remaining majestically erect, never bowing to the idols, policies, and axioms of a godless world but only to the holy will and order of their Lord.

YOUR NOSE IS AS THE TOWER OF LEBANON

While this cameo is not second in the text, we will consider the "*fishpools of Heshbon*" third. In the Shulamite with a countenance as the tower of Lebanon, we have the idea of strength, security, supremacy, prominence, and power. Her face, ever noble and brave, as Stephen's when being martyred for Christ's sake, is set against all seductive forces.

The symbol of the tower can also be used of Israel, indicating the strength and supremacy of the nation during Solomon's reign when nations were at her feet, looking toward Damascus, the capital of a once-powerful foe.

The tower can be likened also to the impregnability of the church, of which her Founder said, "*The gates of hell shall not prevail against* [her]" (Matthew 16:18). Although continually besieged by the dark hatred of the devil, she emerges more formidable than ever. The visible church is certainly "sore oppressed, by schisms rent asunder and by heresies distressed," but the invisible church, composed of all the Bridegroom calls His holy bride, has a mystic sweet communion with their Beloved which nothing can destroy.

YOUR EYES LIKE THE FISHPOOLS IN HESHBON

Artificial lakes or pools were situated in the most populous part of Heshbon. To these charming pools, surrounded and lined with a verdant edging of flowers and lilies, the beloved likened his lovely and attractive spouse. They were suggestive of her calm, deep reflective nature; for her heart, like her eyes, reflected a life undefiled, pure, and clear.

Applied to Israel, the pools can represent Israel's peaceful reign under Solomon, whose name means "peace."

Used of the church, they can indicate how she acts as a guide to blind travelers through a trackless desert, just as the pools of Heshbon were guides to strangers entering the city. Sure guides are referred to as "*eyes*" (Numbers 10:31; Job 29:15).

Location of the Fish Pools

We are told that Heshbon was by the gate of Bathrabbim, the celebrated city of the Amorites beyond Jordan. *Heshbon* means, "he that hastens to understand or build." This is a spur for us to understand the will and word of the Lord and thus, by the Spirit, build up a holy life. As for *Bathrabbim*, this broad gate means "daughter of many" or "a multitude." It was so called because it was the gate of thronged thoroughfare with crowds of people streaming through it, the incessant concourse being gathered from the high places of the city.

Lessons of the Fishpools

This renowned spot is beautifully typical, not only of the Shulamite, but also of Israel and of the church. As the water pools were so charming, calm, and clear, the bride's eyes were as blue and placid as the lake. Truly, there is nothing so attractive, so serene, as the full bright eye of saints as they move through a world of unrest and turmoil.

141

Lesson of Clarity

The first feature, *"eyes like the fishpools in Heshbon,"* is one of clarity and reflectiveness. Here the unruffled water reflects the brightness of the blue heavens above the fleecy clouds. Would that we had eyes reflecting the glory of God, the beauty of the Savior, and the holiness of the Spirit!

What the world too often sees is, alas, somewhat different. Our eyes are hot-tempered looking, or blurred by earthly desire and possessions. May the Lord so enable us to live that as a turbulent world looks into our eyes, it only sees the sweet, clear reflection of heavenly virtues.

If we dwell in
the great
depths of God,
we will not be easily
disturbed or
enmeshed in the
weeds of doubt
or worry.

The secret of a vision unhindered by any cataract is the constant contemplation of the Lord, whose eyes are able to guide us because of their clear, holy vision. *"But we all, with unveiled face, [reflecting] as in a mirror the glory of the Lord, are transformed into the same image from glory to glory, even as from the Lord the Spirit"* (2 Corinthians 3:18 ASV). We can never radiate His image unless He imprints it initially within the innermost parts of our being. Those around will never see in our features a reflection of the blue heaven of peace if ours is a tarnished soul. The secret of clarity of vision is found in the determination of the psalmist, *"My eyes are ever toward the LORD"* (Psalm 25:15).

Lesson of Depth

The tranquil lakes of Heshbon indicate that their water was not shallow, but deep and full; hence they contained a great quantity of fish. Do our eyes suggest that depth of character, of life, of thought, of holiness made possible by the indwelling Spirit? Too many of us are shallow with superficial spiritual experiences, and no fish can live in shallow waters.

The Gospels have the parable of the tragic condition of seed that withered away because it had *"no deepness of earth"* (Matthew 13:5). We must live in the "deeps" of the truths of God, which can give us eyes filled with the depth of God's love—eyes filled with holy thoughts and reflective of living deeper lives. *"Deep calls to deep"* (Psalm 42:7) says the psalmist, and may the deep within us ever call for the deepest in God for our life and witness in a somewhat shallow world.

If pools lack depth, fish soon reach the bottom and die in weeds entangling them. The fishpools of Heshbon were never troubled by sand and mire. Any impurities were excluded, for sluices only admitted pure water. May our eyes never become dim because of any spiritual grit or impurity within. Only the constant inflow of the Spirit can keep our spiritual eyesight clear and clean.

If we dwell in the great depths of God, we will not be easily disturbed or enmeshed in the weeds of doubt or worry. Those who are always busy criticizing and damaging the character of others, raking up the mud, are certainly not dwellers of the deep.

Lesson of Tranquility

An unknown poet expressed this feature of the fishpools, and their lesson, most admirably:

144

> Serene as Heshbon's tranquil lake
> Thy meditative eyes forsake
>   The world's distracting joys.
> Beside its well-stored waters clear
> The City's crowded gates appear,
>   But nought its calm destroys.

Deep though those pools were, they were yet calm and quiet, presenting an unruffled surface. This is not a feature of dreaminess or the other-worldly look some strive to cultivate of the eyes of a hermit in the wilderness or of one secluded in a cloister or convent, but these are pools of Heshbon, the gate of Bath-rabbim, the great marketplace with the busy throng. Despite the crowds, if one is dwelling deep:

> Not a surge of worry
>   Not a shade of care,

Not a blast of hurry,
   Touch the spirit there.[49]

If ours is a serenity and peace independent of all out-ward circumstances and experiences, it is because of the deep, settled peace of God within the heart. *"You will keep him in perfect peace* [ASV margin reads *peace, peace*], *whose mind is stayed on You: because he trusts in You"* (Isaiah 26:3).

God's heavenly Dove alone makes possible the tran-quility whereby we are unperturbed by the adverse hap-penings of life. *"When He gives quietness, who then can make trouble?"* (Job 34:29). It was when Horatius Bonar found himself troubled and harassed that he sat down and wrote:

145

Calm me, my God, and keep me calm,
While these hot breezes blow.[50]

The peace He desires our eyes to reflect is His own peace which He gives His own obedient ones. How assuring are the lines of Jessie Rose Gates in her poem on *Peace*:

There is a peace that cometh after sorrow
Of hope surrendered, not of hope fulfilled:
A peace that looketh not upon tomorrow,
But calmly on a tempest that is stilled.

A peace which lives not now in joy's excesses,
Nor in the happy life of love secure:

49. Francis Ridley Havergal, "Like a River, Glorious," 1876.
50. Horatius Bonar, "Calm Me, My God," 1857.

But in the strength the heart possesses
Of conflicts won while learning to endure.

A peace there is, in Sacrifice secluded,
A life subdued, from will and passions free;
'Tis not the peace which over Eden broodeth,
But which triumphed in Gethsemane.

What a beautiful picture of peace is the gospel narrative of Jesus asleep in a tempest-driven boat. In the middle of raging forces without and around, He was yet calm and peaceful, for He was asleep in God. When awake, His two eyes were like miniature heavens reflecting God, so much so that He could say, *"He that has seen Me has seen the Father"* (John 14:9). The Savior's eyes were the deep eyes of the God-Man because there was nothing shallow, superficial, or unreal about His perfect life. Amid the hostile voices and foes, and innumerable sorrows, He remained unruffled and undisturbed and now offers in His tranquility, *"My peace I give to you"* (John 14:27).

If you hear our Beloved ask, *"What will you that I shall do to you?"* (Luke 18:41), may your quick answer be, "Lord, that I might receive sight, and have eyes reflecting Thy lovely image and beauty!"

So in this stillness Thou beholdest only
Thine image in the waters of my breast.[51]

---

51. Harriet Beecher Stowe.

Chapter 15

UNDER THE APPLE TREE

The closing chapter of the Song of Solomon seems to recapitulate the principles of the book and contains some of the most magnificent descriptions of pure love ever written. It ends (as people like such stories of pure love to) sweetly, beautifully, and naturally. It typifies the perfect bliss of the believer's life.

> Who is this that comes up from the wilderness, leaning upon her beloved? I raised you up under the apple tree: there your mother brought you forth: there she brought you forth that bore you. Set me as a seal upon your heart, as a seal upon your arm: for love is strong as death; jealousy is cruel as the grave: the coals thereof are coals of fire, which has a most vehement flame. Many waters cannot quench love, neither can the floods drown it: if a man would give all the substance of his house for love, it would utterly be contemned. (Song of Solomon 8:5–7)

Ellicott comments on the above verses:

This fine passage with its reference to the invincible might and untempted constancy of true love hardly leaves in doubt that the poem, while an ideal picture of the passion, is also a reminiscence of an actual history of two hearts that had been tried and proved true both against difficulties and seductions.

We will consider three phrases from these verses.

UP FROM THE WILDERNESS: COMPANIONSHIP

The companions of the shepherd-lover who witnessed his return with the Shulamite probably asked the question, *"Who is this that comes up from the wilderness, leaning upon her beloved?"* (8:5). Tender and expressive, this question suggests the believer's pilgrimage and the believer's prospect.

The Believer's Pilgrimage

"Up from the wilderness" aptly describes our weary pilgrimage through the world in which we live. God said of Israel, *"He found him in a desert land, and in the waste howling wilderness"* (Deuteronomy 32:10; see Acts 7:30). Those of the church *"confessed that they were strangers and pilgrims on the earth"* (Hebrews 11:13).

It will be observed that actually the beloved was returning from Solomon's court and presence, yet it is spoken of as a *"wilderness."* No matter how attractive and magnificent it may appear, the world is a wilderness without Christ. Everything in the world is stained with sin, and fades, yet we are kept in it that we might win deluded souls around us for our heavenly Beloved. The Lord is able to cause the wilderness to blossom for us.

The Believer's Prospect

The emphasis is upon *"up."* The Shulamite and her beloved were seen coming up together out of the wilderness. Is not the life of the saint one of ascent? We sing "Marching up to Zion," and day by day we draw nearer to our eternal home. Robert Murray McCheyne could say that "Sabbath days are the milestones marking our way."

This wilderness is not our rest, for before long our Beloved will say, *"Arise you, and depart; for this is not your rest: because it is polluted"* (Micah 2:10). Saints of old *"looked for a city which has foundations, whose builder and maker is God"* (Hebrews 11:10). Their eyes were upward, and the day came when they went up to meet the Builder. Paul made clear the ascension of believers when he wrote that they are to be caught up together to meet the Lord in the air. (See 1 Thessalonians 4:17.) May we cultivate the upward life and look!

The Believer's Privilege and Posture

What a tender touch is the description of the spouse coming up through the wilderness leaning upon her beloved! Micah wrote of those who *"lean[ed] upon the LORD"* (Micah 3:11). John, the disciple whom Jesus loved, is spoken of as leaning on his Master's bosom. (See John 13:23; 21:20.) How privileged we are to have the same beloved One to lean upon as we go through the wilderness of this life! We are not only going up to Him, but here and now we can walk and talk with Him and rest upon Him. Solomon advises us not to lean upon our

149

Christ's love

affords shadow and fruit for all those He awakened, or raised, or brought forth by His Spirit.

own understanding, but to trust in the Lord with all our heart, or lean our entire weight upon Him alone. (See Proverbs 3:5.) Our privileged posture is epitomized in the popular hymn from *Redemption Songs*:

> What a fellowship, what a joy divine,
> Leaning on the everlasting arms;
> What a blessedness, what a peace is mine,
> Leaning on the everlasting arms.
>
> Oh, how sweet to walk in this pilgrim way,
> Leaning on the everlasting arms;
> O how bright the path grows from day to day,
> Leaning on the everlasting arms.
>
> What have I to dread, what have I to fear,
> Leaning on the everlasting arms?
> I have blessed peace with my Lord so near,
> Leaning on the everlasting arms.[52]

The LXX version has the addition, "Who is this that cometh up from the wilderness *"all white,"* while the Vulgate version puts it, *"flowing with delights."* So this verse also represents the church, His bride, taken up from the wilderness of the world *"all white"* or as pure as the Bridegroom himself and "flowing with delights" at the prospect of being with Him forever.

UNDER THE APPLE TREE: GRACE

It was under the apple tree, the birthplace of their love, that the two lovers pledged their troth. The maiden has said of

---

52. Elisha A. Hoffman, "Leaning on the Everlasting Arms," 1887.

her lover, "*As the apple-tree among the trees of the wood, so is my beloved among the sons. I sat under his shadow with great delight, and his fruit was sweet to my taste*" (2:3). "*I raised you up*" and I "*brought you forth*" are phrases suggesting all the Lord is to His own, affording shadow and fruit for all those He awakened, or raised, or brought forth by His Spirit. Provision is all from His side, with grace and redemption originating with Him.

Whether it was fruit from an apple tree Satan tempted Eve with, and which, yielding to the seducer, she gave to Adam, Scripture does not say. Thomas Hood, nineteenth-century poet, followed the idea of the proverbial apple in his whimsical way in the stanza:

When Eve upon the first of Men
The apple press'd with specious cant
Oh! What a thousand pities then
That Adam was not Adamant.

Yet there was grace in Eden, for near that historic tree God gave the world the first promise of salvation from the sin introduced into the world by the forbidden fruit. The early fathers saw in the *apple tree* a type of the cross, referred to by the early church as the *tree* upon which Jesus was hanged. (See Acts 5:30; 10:39; Galatians 3:13; 1 Peter 2:24.) Although to Him the tree was the emblem of shame, suffering, and sacrifice, yet to the believer it is *the tree* among the trees of the wood because its fruit is full salvation, true love, and abundant joy. That "old rugged tree" exhausted the curse pronounced at Eden's tree and bears fruit gladdening the heart of both God and man. It was at the cross we first saw the light and where the Spirit awakened us and brought us forth.

152

UPON YOUR HEART: LOVE

No greater panegyric of true love can be found in the entire realm of literature than that Solomon puts into the mouth of the beloved to describe the unquenchable, unconquerable love of the Shulamite in verses six and seven of this concluding chapter of the Song. Four outstanding features of the supreme love of Christ are symbolized: love that is boundless, love that is a seal upon our arms, love that is as strong as death, and love that is quenchless.

Love That Is Boundless

We will never be able to fully understand the height, depth, breadth, and length of Christ's love that passes knowledge, and which calls us into holy intimacy with Himself.

> There is no love like the love of Jesus,
> Never to fade or fall,
> Till into the rest of the house of God
> He has gathered us all.[53]

The double mention of "*seal*" indicates something especially dear and precious. It also represents a finished transaction. "*Set me as a seal upon your heart*" (Song of Solomon 8:6).

As a ring of seals was bound around the neck, or carried on the bosom (see Genesis 38:18–25; Haggai 2:23), so the spouse wanted to be as near to her lover as possible. The high priest's beautiful jeweled breastplate upon which was sealed the names of the twelve tribes typifies our Great High Priest who has us upon His heart. May we constantly pray: "Let my name be written upon Thy breastplate, near to Thy heart. Hide me deeper, bind me closer, draw me nearer, carry me more completely, O Lord."

53. W. E. Littlewood, "There Is No Love Like the Love of Jesus," 1857.

To Christ, the *tree* was the emblem of shame, suffering, and sacrifice, yet to the *believer* its fruit is full *salvation*, true *love*, and abundant *joy*.

Love As a Seal upon Your Arm

The previous aspect was inward, "*your heart*," but this is outward, "*your arm*." A seal on the Lord's arm betokens authority and power made visible on behalf of those who rest in His love. The high priest also had two precious stones on the two shoulders or arms of his garment. (See Exodus 28:11–12.) The saint is but a child and needs not only to be loved, but guarded and carried. Looked at from another angle, the twofold sealing can indicate two things. If we are sealed as the Lord's, then we must bear the impress of His character. All parts of our life must be stamped with His seal. (See 2 Timothy 2:19.) In the sanctuary of old, even the pots carried the imprint of holiness. (See Zechariah 14:21.) When we became the Lord's, the sealing with the Holy Spirit was His initial act, and such inward sealing is necessary before there can be power in service. *Heart*, then the *arm*.

155

Love That Is Strong as Death (Deathless)

When associated with the Shulamite, the inference is most appealing. Death claims its own in the long run, but she will never let her lover go, for his love for her, and hers for him, is irresistible and will continue till death and beyond it. Death is terribly strong and attacks the stoutest, bringing them down in a moment of time. The strong, immortal love of our Beloved can also break the hardest heart, as it did that of Saul of Tarsus on the Damascus Road. His love ever conquers because it is the strength of Himself. In this way…

Life shall be transformed to love,
A heaven below, and heaven above.

In "*jealousy is cruel as the grave*," the word for *jealousy* implies "to be red with flame" and represents passion, not in a bad sense, but good, as the parallelism of the verse shows. Love and jealousy have an irresistible power over those brought under their sway and dominion. As none can escape the grave, the place of the dead, so none can escape from the arms of true, deep love. The grave is stubborn and will not give up its own, and the Shulamite, in spite of seductive efforts to woo her from her beloved, would not surrender him for another.

Scripture makes it clear that we have a choice between two eternal fires: "*Who shall separate us from the love of Christ?*" (Romans 8:35); "*Whosoever was not found written in the book of life was cast into the lake of fire*" (Revelation 20:15).

156   God is a jealous God, and the love of His Son is a jealous love. No idol can be tolerated by divine love, the reality and warmth of which is eternal, loving unto the end. Two parts of a whole, then, are here emphasized: toward us the love of God is as strong as death; toward everything not of Himself, it's as cruel as the grave.

> Break through my nature, mighty, heavenly love,
> Clear every avenue of thought and brain,
> Flood my affections, purify my will,
> Let nothing but Thine own pure life remain.[54]

Love That Is Quenchless

See what an abundance of arresting metaphors Solomon marshaled to illustrate the high qualities of true love!

---

54. Emily May Grimes, "Thy Mighty Love, O God, Constraineth Me," date unknown.

The flashes thereof are flashes of fire,
A very flame of Jehovah.
Many waters cannot quench love,
Neither can floods drown it:
If a man would give all the substance of his house for love,
He would utterly be contemned.

(Song of Solomon 8:6–7 ASV)

A Most Vehement Flame

"*Flashes of fire*" and the "*flame of Jehovah*" speak of love's consuming power. An old translator put it, "The fire-flame of God." Such was the nature of the love binding the beloved and his spouse together as one. It was fierce and resistless. The love of God is an inextinguishable flame, perpetually passionate and compassionate. "*I have loved you with an everlasting love*" (Jeremiah 31:3). Its flashes of fire quickly burn up all chaff and dross within the heart. It is also a love warming the cold heart, until it glows like a fire.

157

Time, that affects all things below,
Can never change the love He'll show:
And in the present of to-day.
Forever loved.[55]

Many Waters Cannot Quench Love

This passage may relate to the experiences of the Shulamite whom Solomon tried to entice to become part of his famous harem. The waters of flattery, attraction, and seduction could not transfer or quench her love of the beloved. Nor could

55. Grace Pennell.

anything quench the love of Jesus for His Father and for mankind, even though He passed through the waters of death. Oh that we might have the same unquenchable love for Him, constraining us to say with Job, *"Though He slay me, yet will I trust in Him"* (Job 13:15).

Neither Can the Floods Drown It

In the same way the enemy came "in like a flood," Solomon probably did in a last attempt to allure the maiden, but she remained true to her beloved. The floods of man's sin and rejection could not overwhelm or bury Christ's love toward sinners, for, while they were yet sinners, He loved them and died for their salvation.

Whole seas of trouble cannot quench
  Love's everlasting fire:
Though Hell oppose whom I have chosen
  I cannot but admire;
Earthly things cannot destroy that which is Divine.

Love That Is Priceless

Solomon failed to buy the love of the Shulamite. Her lowly shepherd-lover had nothing to give her but himself, and she was blissfully content to love him for what he *was*, not what he *had*. Therefore, it was easy for her to reject all that Solomon offered for her affection. No man could possibly purchase the love of the Lord, even if he offered all his substance. He never sells such love but urges us to be saved by its sacrifice. (See Romans 5:7–8.)

The Lord desires our love, our very selves, before any substance that we can offer, as Paul reminds us. (See 1 Corinthians 13.)

Thomas Kempis would have us remember that "he that loveth, giveth all for all, and hath all in all."

While there are many other metaphors of true love in the Song, sufficient have been used to show that our heavenly Beloved is the fountain and channel of an eternal love that will not let us go, and which, in turn, desires and demands undivided and ever-deepening love.

May we have the like-passion of Madame Guyon, expressed in her appealing lines:

Why have I not a thousand, thousand hearts,
  Lord of my soul! that they might all be thine?
If thou approve,—the zeal thy smile imparts,
  How should it ever fail! can such a fire decline?
Love, pure and holy, is a deathless fire;
  Its object heavenly, it must ever blaze:
Eternal love a God must needs inspire,
  When once he wins the heart, and fits it for his praise.[56]

159

---

56. Madame Guyon, William Cowper, trans., "God Neither Known Nor Loved By the World, *The Complete Poetical Works of William Cowper* (London: Henry G. Bohn, 1849), 630.

ABOUT THE AUTHOR

When Dr. Herbert Lockyer (1886–1984) was first deciding on a career, he considered becoming an actor. Tall and well-spoken, he seemed a natural for the theater. But the Lord had something better in mind. Instead of the stage, God called Herbert to the pulpit, where, as a pastor, a Bible teacher, and the author of more than fifty books, he touched the hearts and lives of millions of people.

Dr. Lockyer held pastorates in Scotland and England for twenty-five years. As pastor of Leeds Road Baptist Church in Bradford, England, he became a leader in the Keswick Higher Life Movement, which emphasized the significance of living in the fullness of the Holy Spirit. This led to an invitation to speak at the Moody Bible Institute's fiftieth anniversary in 1936. His warm reception at that event led to his ministry in the United States. He received honorary degrees from both the Northwestern Evangelical Seminary and the International Academy in London.

In 1955, he returned to England, where he lived for many years. He then returned to the United States, where he spent the final years of his life in Colorado Springs, Colorado, with his son, the Rev. Herbert Lockyer Jr., a Presbyterian minister who eventually became his editor.